Praise for Na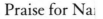

'The testimonies of 14 women collected in *White Torture* read like a charge sheet against the Islamic Republic. Fortunately for future prosecutors, this book is full of inquisitors' names. Should the ayatollahs and their bully boys fall, it will surely form part of the case against them. And, as it did for Mr Khamenei, the torment of Iran's prisons might yet propel their inmates to power.'

Economist

'The testimonies of these brave women are made more effective for being delivered in Amir Rezanezhad's calm, understated translation. They reveal an awe-inspiring capacity for resilience and resistance . . . Their courage is beyond imagination.'

Irish Times

'Ms Mohammadi's research from prison, based on interviewing inmates, resulted in a book about the emotional impact of solitary confinement and prison conditions in Iran.'

New York Times

'These women reveal the truth about the Islamic Republic and they pay the price for it. Through reading their testimonials we too learn the truth. The question every reader should ask herself is, now that we know the truth, what are we going to do about it?'

Azar Nafisi, author of *Reading Lolita in Tehran*

White Torture

Interviews with Iranian Women Prisoners

Narges Mohammadi

Translated by Amir Rezanezhad

ONEWORLD

A Oneworld Book

First published in English by Oneworld Publications in 2022
This paperback edition published 2023
First published in Persian by Baran Publishing
(Sweden) under the title *Shekanje Sefid* in 2020

ISBN 978-0-86154-876-7
eISBN 978-0-86154-551-3

Typeset by Hewer Text UK Ltd, Edinburgh
Printed and bound in Great Britain by Clays Ltd, Elcograf S.p.A.

Oneworld Publications
10 Bloomsbury Street
London WC1B 3SR
England

Stay up to date with the latest books,
special offers, and exclusive content from
Oneworld with our newsletter

Sign up on our website
oneworld-publications.com

MIX
Paper from
responsible sources
FSC® C018072

CONTENTS

Narges Mohammadi's Letter to the Norwegian Nobel Committee   vii

Preface by Narges Mohammadi   xiii

Foreword by Shirin Ebadi   xv

A Note on Narges Mohammadi by Nayereh Tohidi   xxi

Introduction by Shannon Woodcock   1

INTERVIEWS AND TESTIMONIES

Narges Mohammadi   15

Nigara Afsharzadeh   51

Atena Daemi   63

Zahra Zahtabchi   75

Nazanin Zaghari-Ratcliffe   91

Mahvash Shahriari   113

Hengameh Shahidi   137

Reyhaneh Tabatabai 157

Sima Kiani 167

Fatemeh Mohammadi 175

Sedigheh Moradi 183

Nazila Nouri and Shokoufeh Yadollahi 199

Marzieh Amiri 209

Postscript: Updates on the Women Interviewed 229

Index 233

NARGES MOHAMMADI'S LETTER TO THE NORWEGIAN NOBEL COMMITTEE

Dear Chair and members of the Nobel Committee,

I thank the Norwegian Nobel Committee for their clear and profound recognition of the power and impact of the people's protests in Iran's recent revolutionary and social uprisings.

In an attempt to denounce the award, the Islamic Republic's media broadcast the official announcement in the Women's Section of Evin Prison. As soon as Berit Reiss-Andersen, chair of the committee, began with the words '*Zan, Zendegi, Azadi*' ('Woman, Life, Freedom'), I heard my cellmates' exultant cries echoing that powerful slogan. Their voices fused together, reverberating with the 'protesting power' of Iranians around the world.

The potent waves of this slogan, heard in two locations far from each other at the same significant historical moment, spoke of the vast and formidable power of the people and their decisive role in today's global political climate.

The laudable decision of the committee to start the announcement by referring to Iran's revolutionary movement was a turning point in empowering all the social and protest movements around the world to become the key forces to bring about fundamental change in today's societies. Honouring a defender of human rights with this award gives all these movements special significance.

We in the Middle East, particularly those of us living in Iran and Afghanistan, do not learn about the importance of freedom, democracy and human rights from theories in textbooks, but through our personal experience of oppression and discrimination. We have come to understand the importance of these concepts, and have risen up against their violators and adversaries, because from childhood, in our daily lives, we have faced oppression, open and subtle violence, harassment and discrimination by authoritarian governments.

When I was only nine years old, I heard my mother wailing, mourning the execution of her nephew, a young student. I heard my grandmother weeping at the torture of her son. Back then, I had no idea what 'execution' or 'torture' meant. My childish illusions were ruthlessly torn apart.

No one heard the voices of the mothers seeking justice in the 1980s, a decade that saw widespread execution, torture, rape and assault in prisons. One of its main perpetrators was Ebrahim Raisi, the current president of the Islamic Republic. Despotism, hiding behind the mask of religion, imposed repression, domination, and widespread poverty and misery on Iran.

When I was nineteen, I was arrested for wearing an orange

coat. In the detention centre with dozens of other women who had been arrested, I was shocked and utterly horrified to see whips in the hands of angry men in black who were viciously lashing four women, without any legal process.

Years later, in 2022, a young woman named Mahsa (Jina) Amini, who was wearing both a coat and headscarf, was arrested on the pretext of her inadequate hijab, and within hours lost her life while still in custody. Hundreds of protesters took to the streets and were blinded by bullets, hundreds more were killed, and six protesters were executed. A flood of arrests of women and protesters ensued, followed by torture, solitary confinement, assault and sexual harassment. Universities were attacked by thuggish security forces. Civic organizations and activists were increasingly suppressed, and even the families of those seeking justice for their loved ones were thrown into jail.

I declare that the reason for Islamic Republic's imposition of compulsory hijab is not its concern for religious rules, social customs and traditions or, as it claims, the safeguarding of women's reputations.

Instead, it openly aims to oppress and dominate women in this way as a means of dominating Iranian society as a whole. It has legalized and systematized this tyranny and the repression of women. The women of Iran will no longer accept this.

The compulsory hijab is an instrument of domination. It serves to prolong the reign of 'religious despotism'. For forty-five years this government has institutionalized poverty and deprivation in our country. This regime is based on lies, deception and intimidation, and with its destabilizing and warmongering policies, it has seriously threatened peace and calm in the region and in the world.

In today's Iran, women and youth make up the most radical, progressive and significant social force both fighting religious tyranny and seeking fundamental change to achieve a durable peace in Iran, the Middle East and the world.

The world knows that this new revolutionary movement of 'Woman, Life, Freedom' is a continuation of the ongoing political resistance in Iran, the struggle to re-establish normal life in society. The strength of this movement lies in the agency of Iranian women. We clearly know 'what we want' better than 'what we don't want'. We are committed to it, we believe in it, and we are certain of our ultimate victory.

We, the people of Iran, demand democracy, freedom, human rights and equality. The Islamic Republic is the main obstacle for the realization of the collective will of the people. Our determination is unwavering. We are attempting to exercise solidarity and power in a non-violent and unstoppable process to transition away from a tyrannical religious government, and restore glory and honour to Iran, making it worthy of its people.

Finally, speaking from Evin's Women's Section, surrounded by political prisoners and prisoners of conscience, including long-serving women prisoners with a variety of political and intellectual viewpoints, Bahá'ís in prison for their beliefs, environmental activists, public intellectuals, the passionate women protesters of the Mahsa/Jina movement, journalists and students, I send my most sincere greetings and gratitude to the Norwegian Nobel Committee, with a heart full of love, hope and passion.

I want to also extend my gratitude to the following: the global media; journalists who carry our voices out into the world; feminists of the world who consider women's rights to be a litmus test of democracy, peace and the quality of life, and push the world to always change for the better; human rights bodies that are a sanctuary for humanity; Amnesty International; civic communities; networks and organizations of social movements; 'the people', who are the ultimate authority; distinguished thinkers and politicians who consider human rights and peace a necessity for politics; artists who show the world a real picture of what's happening in Iran, Afghanistan and the Middle East; writers; PEN International; Nobel Peace laureates including Ms Shirin Ebadi; all my colleagues in Iranian NGOs; my cellmates over the long years in prison; the unnamed and unknown women who came onto the streets to protest, and in this way became the embodiment of resistance; the mothers seeking justice; my family, Kiana and Ali; and finally all those who congratulated me for this award. Thank you all. I ask you to support the people of Iran until our final victory.

Our victory will not be easy, but it is certain.

Narges Mohammadi
Evin Prison
October 2023

PREFACE

I am writing this preface in the final hours of my home leave. Very soon I will be forced to return to prison.

On 16 November 2021, I was arrested for the twelfth time and sentenced to solitary confinement for the fourth time in my life. I spent sixty-four days in confinement in Ward 209 of Evin Prison, run by the Islamic Republic of Iran's Ministry of Intelligence. This time I was found guilty because of the book you are holding in your hands – *White Torture*. They accused me of blackening the name of Iran across the world. Now they were determined to prove that my campaign to end solitary confinement had failed. Once again they would subject me to this torture and demonstrate to activists all over the globe that the government reigns supreme.

I was illegally sentenced to eight years and two months in prison, and seventy-four lashes by the primary court, which was subsequently commuted to six years in prison, with the same number of lashes. As a result, I am serving two separate sentences: a prior one of thirty months in prison and eighty lashes, as well as this recent one. When taken together with an earlier sentence, I now face over thirty years in prison.

But nothing will stop me from continuing my struggle against solitary confinement. Having been granted temporary release due to my poor health following a heart attack in Qarchak Prison and cardiac surgery, I declare once more that this is a cruel and inhumane punishment. I will not rest until it is abolished.

They will put me behind bars again. But I will not stop campaigning until human rights and justice prevail in my country.

Narges Mohammadi
March 2022

FOREWORD

White Torture is a collection of twelve interviews that the compassionate activist Narges Mohammadi conducted with women in her own agonizing situation. Since the 2009 presidential election, Narges has been repeatedly imprisoned for her activities as the vice president and spokesperson of the Defenders of Human Rights Center. This organization campaigns for the abolition of the death penalty.

She is now confined in Zanjan Prison, a confinement which is illegal even by the laws of the Islamic Republic. The reason for this imprisonment lies in her sympathy for the conditions endured by other prisoners. Many protesters had been killed in nationwide anti-government demonstrations in November 2019. Commemorating the fortieth day after their deaths and as an act of solidarity with their families, Narges intended to conduct a sit-down strike with other inmates. She had courageously informed the authorities and the public that this strike would be held in the office of the women's ward of Evin Prison in Tehran. On the third day, claiming that her lawyer was going to meet her, the head of the prison summoned Narges to his office. Gholmarza Ziaei, the head of the prison, verbally abused Narges and threatened her with death. She wordlessly turned away to head back to her cell. Ziaei slammed Narges into the wall and brutally beat her, bruising her body and smashing her hands through a glass door, causing them to bleed. Despite her injuries, the authorities immediately transferred Narges to Zanjan Prison. She filed a complaint in December 2019 against the head of the prison, which was deliberately ignored. Curiously enough, Ziaei filed a complaint against Narges for 'libel against the head of the prison' in retaliation.

Contrary to the law regulating criminal procedures and because of this complaint, an investigator came to the prison to question and talk to Narges. She asked him why they would not summon her to the Zanjan courthouse so that she could answer their questions like everyone else, including ordinary prisoners. 'You're not allowed to leave the prison under any circumstances,' he said. 'That's why we've come here to question you.'

'I will not answer your questions here either,' she replied, objecting to his illegal actions.

Two more cases against Narges are currently being investigated in addition to the existing convictions. The security officer in charge of Narges' case has told her multiple times that she would be immediately released if she ceased campaigning and resigned from the Defenders of Human Rights Center. Narges rejected the offer. An official from the

Ministry of Intelligence threatened her, saying 'Then rest assured that you won't get out of prison alive.'

In Zanjan, Narges has not always been kept safe from her fellow prisoners. A while ago, some of these prisoners approached Narges at the instigation of prison guards, who'd promised them early leave and release if they dealt with her. Narges hid in the bathroom all night after one of the prisoners threatened to kill her. Fortunately, the government's plan failed and Narges, due to her good character and the legal aid she provided to the prison's homeless women, gradually became friends with other prisoners and got through this crisis.

Now Covid-19 has spread all over the world, including in Iran and especially in its prisons. One of Narges' cellmates was diagnosed with Covid-19 and was sent home. A few days later other cellmates, including Narges, began to display symptoms, but prison officials denied them the right to be tested. As their conditions worsened and their families put pressure on prison authorities, they were eventually tested. Nevertheless, the officials refused to inform Narges of her results.

Only four cellmates, who showed no signs of the disease, were released. Narges and eleven other inmates remain isolated in quarantine. Even though Narges is at greater risk, as she suffers from pulmonary embolism and muscular paralysis, prison officials do not allow her to see her own specialist. They claim that the prison's healthcare centre suffices. Yet everyone knows Iranian prisons' healthcare facilities are limited, particularly in Zanjan.

Narges has informed the authorities and the public about these unjust conditions. She even asked the health minister to come to the prison to see the inadequate healthcare for himself. Instead of meeting her demands, the chief of staff of the judiciary derided her as a liar and said that the information provided by her was not verified by the chief of Zanjan Prison.

No prison wall has been able to prevent the voice of Narges Mohammadi from reaching the people. When she found out in Evin Prison that women prisoners, unlike men, did not have the right to make telephone calls to their relatives and children, she called for a special campaign to 'support mothers in prison'. This campaign attracted the attention of Iranians around the world and forced the government to retreat. As a result, women were given the right to make calls. On this basis, Narges could talk to her two children (although only for twenty-four minutes a week) who live in exile in Paris with their father. Later, when the government took note of Narges' tenacity in protesting against injustice and supporting others, her right to make calls was removed. It is now about a year since she last heard the voices of her children. As she wrote in a letter, 'I do not know if my children will know me when I come out in the coming years. Will they recognize my voice? Will they call me mother again?'

Narges has now served more than seven years of her ten-year sentence and technically is eligible for parole, but she is deprived of the rights of an ordinary prisoner. They can buy meat, vegetables or fruit from the prison store, but she is forbidden. So, Narges has eaten only the daily rations for prisoners since her move to Zanjan Prison: potatoes, eggs and bread.

As you can see, despite the chains in which she has been placed, Narges still roars like a lioness. This is why the regime wants to crush her.

White Torture is another roar of this lioness. The central subject of these interviews is the use of solitary confinement in Iranian prisons, one of the most prominent examples of torture. Narges Mohammadi has always been the flag bearer of opposition to solitary confinement even before she was imprisoned. She has continued to resist solitary confinement while incarcerated.

To express her opposition, she has conducted interviews with a number of her inmates, namely the prisoners of conscience incarcerated alongside her.

When people recall their experiences after a few years have passed, parts of them are inevitably forgotten or merged with other memories. That is why these immediate records are so important.

These statements were made there and then, within the prison walls, and are a testament to the efforts to secure justice for prisoners of conscience in Iran.

This is the accomplishment of Narges Mohammadi who, despite every hardship, understands this need to bear witness and does not abandon her goals.

It is excruciating to see a person imprisoned for their human rights activism, and watch them being deprived of all the legal rights that even the Islamic regime grants to ordinary prisoners, because they won't remain silent in the face of injustice. Our history won't let Narges and all these lionesses be consigned to the ether.

Shirin Ebadi
July 2020

A NOTE ON NARGES MOHAMMADI

Narges Mohammadi is one of Iran's most dedicated representatives of civil and human rights; a leading anti-death penalty campaigner; a pre-eminent advocate of women's rights; the vice president of the National Council for Peace; and the vice president and spokeswoman for the Defenders of Human Rights Center (DHRC).

Narges has been one of the most courageous and outspoken prisoners of conscience in the Islamic Republic of Iran. Her persistent, non-violent resistance against what she calls 'tyranny' and her defiance of oppressive laws and policies for twenty-eight years now, inside and outside prison, has earned her respect nationally and internationally. After several arrests and many years of incarceration following each, her last arrest resulted in a sixteen-year sentence of imprisonment, ten years of which she had to serve.

Narges suffers from neurological and pulmonary conditions, putting her at high risk of complications if infected with Covid-19. In July 2020, a group of United Nations human rights experts called for her release, citing reports that she was showing Covid-19 symptoms. 'For those with underlying health conditions, such as Ms. Mohammadi, it may have life-or-death consequences,' they wrote. 'The Iranian authorities must act now before it is too late.'[1] Thanks to the outcry, the authorities commuted her sentence due to ongoing concerns about her health, exacerbated by the spread of Covid-19 infection throughout the overcrowded prisons in Iran. She was finally released on 7 October 2020 after eight and a half years behind bars.

Alongside the UN human rights experts, several human rights organizations, Iranian and international, had condemned the baseless and illegitimate incarceration of Narges Mohammadi and had called for her immediate release, including Amnesty International, Human Rights Watch, the Observatory for the Protection of Human Rights Defenders, The Nobel Women Initiative, Reporters Without Borders, PEN International and the Iranian Center for Human Rights Defenders. What follows is an outline of Narges' life.

Narges was born on 21 April 1972 in the city of Zanjan in a middle-class family. She studied physics at the International Imam Khomeini University in Qazvin. During her time in

---

1 Maryam Berger, Oct. 8, 2020: Leading Iranian human rights advocate freed from prison amid fear of contracting coronavirus behind bars:
https://www.washingtonpost.com/world/2020/10/08/narges-mohammadi-released-from-prison-iran-coronavirus-human-rights-death-penalty

college, Narges became involved in student activism for the cause of human rights and social justice. She was engaged in the formation of a student organization called *Tashakkol Daaneshjuyi Roshangaraan* ('Enlightened Student Group') and wrote articles in support of students' rights and women's issues in the organization's paper. She was arrested twice during her student years, a prelude to the longer terms of incarceration in her later life.

After graduating, Narges worked as a professional engineer with the Iran Engineering Inspection Corporation. Alongside this, she continued writing in some reformist publications and newspapers, highlighting concerns related to gender equality and democracy in Iran. She also published a book of political essays titled *The Reforms, the Strategy, and the Tactics*. Since the early 1990s, Narges has been a persistent and active advocate for human rights, rule of law and democracy in Iran. She has been a leading member of the feminist movement as well as a strong voice against all forms of discriminations based on gender, sexuality, ethnicity, religion and class differences.

Chronology of imprisonment, separation from her family and resistance

In 1998, Narges Mohammadi was arrested for her criticisms of Iran's government and spent a year in prison. In 1999, she married Taghi Rahmani, a pro-reform journalist who was also a committed activist along the lines of the New Religious Thinkers. But soon after their marriage, Taghi was arrested many times and ended up incarcerated for a total of fourteen years. In 2007, Narges and Taghi became parents of twins, Ali and Kiana. In 2012, during his brief time outside prison, Taghi found out that four new cases had been opened against him – and so he faced another imminent arrest with a long-term sentence. He chose to flee Iran and take refuge in France, a very tough decision. Narges, however, remained in Iran to take care of their children and continue her human rights work. This was a difficult decision for Narges:

> During 2009–2012, I was under pressure by the security agents to leave Iran. They would call my mobile phone directly, and even tell me we can instruct you how to escape Iran by walking through the mountains in Kurdistan in west Iran. I could sense that this was a trap to get rid of my presence in Iran. I naturally refused, arguing that my two children are too small to walk through that rough terrain. After Taghi had to escape to Europe, they called me saying now you have no excuse to stay in Iran, why do not you flee and join your husband? But in recent years, they have not asked me to leave Iran.[2]

It seems obvious that the security agents involved in her case regarded Narges as a serious challenge and preferred to get rid of her by a forced exile or even an assassination during a staged scene of escape. But Narges insisted she would stay

2 From author's online conversation with Narges Mohammadi, 26 April 2021.

despite all the intimidation. A few years later, Narges and Taghi decided that it would be better for the twins to leave Iran to live with their father in exile after Narges was arrested again and was regularly imprisoned.

Maintaining an engineering career while writing and speaking out against human rights violations proved untenable under the repressive system of the Islamic Republic. In 2009, Narges was dismissed from her position with the Engineering Inspection Corporation. In April 2010, she was summoned to the Islamic Revolutionary Court for being a member of the Defenders of Human Rights Center (DHRC). She was released briefly on bail (equivalent to $50,000) but was re-arrested several days later and detained in Evin Prison. While in custody, her health declined, and she developed an epilepsy-like disease causing her to periodically lose muscle control. After a month, she was released and allowed to go to the hospital.

In July 2011, Narges was prosecuted again, and found guilty of 'acting against the national security, membership of the DHRC, and propaganda against the regime (*nezam*)'. In September 2011, she was sentenced to eleven years' imprisonment. As Narges has stated, she learned of the verdict only through her lawyers and was 'given an unprecedented 23-page judgment issued by the court in which they repeatedly likened my human rights activities to attempts to topple the regime'. In March 2012, the sentence was upheld by an appeals court, though it was reduced to six years. On 26 April 2012, she was arrested to begin her sentence.[3]

Many individuals and organizations protested this sentence, including the British Foreign Office, which called it 'another sad example of the Iranian authorities' attempts to silence brave human rights defenders'. Amnesty International designated her a prisoner of conscience and called for her immediate release. Reporters Without Borders issued an appeal on Mohammadi's behalf on the ninth anniversary of photographer Zahra Kazemi's death in Evin Prison, stating that Mohammadi was a prisoner whose life, like that of Zahra Kazemi, was 'in particular danger'. In July 2012, an international group of lawmakers called for her release, including US Senator Mark Kirk, former Canadian Attorney General Irwin Cotler, UK MP Denis MacShane, Australian MP Michael Danby, Italian MP Fiamma Nirenstein and Lithuanian MP Emanuelis Zingeris.

Thanks to this extensive campaigning, Narges Mohammadi was released from prison on 31 July 2012.

These repeated incarcerations could not deter Narges from speaking out against injustice. On 31 October 2014, she made a moving speech at the graveside of Sattar Beheshti, a blogger beaten to death while in custody. In this speech, Narges stated, 'How is it that the Parliament Members are

3 Saeed Kamali Dehghan, 'Iranian Human Rights Activist Narges Mohammadi arrested'. *Guardian*, 26 April 2012, www.theguardian.com/world/iran-blog/2012/apr/26/iran-activist-narges-mohammadi-jailed?newsfeed=true (accessed 27 April 2021).

suggesting a Plan for the Promotion of Virtue and Prevention of Vice, but nobody spoke up two years ago, when an innocent human being by the name of Sattar Beheshti died from torture in the hands of his interrogator?'

Despite the act of extreme violence against Beheshti, which was met with an international uproar back in 2012, his case remains unresolved. Unjust arrests and torture of human rights activists continues to take place today at Evin Prison.

The video of Narges Mohammadi's 31 October speech went viral on social media networks resulting in her being summoned again to Evin Prison court. 'In the summons I received on 5 November 2014, it is stated that I must turn myself in "for charges", but there is no further explanation about these charges,' Narges stated.[4]

On 5 May 2015, Mohammadi was arrested again on account of new charges. Branch 15 of the Revolutionary Court sentenced her to ten years' imprisonment on the charge of 'founding an illegal group', that is, the campaign LEGAM (the Campaign for Step by Step Abolition of the Death Penalty), five years for 'assembly and collusion against national security', a year for 'propaganda against the system' for her interviews with international media, and her meeting with the EU's then High Representative for Foreign Affairs and Security Policy, Catherine Ashton who was visiting Tehran in March 2014.

4 'Iran: Judicial Harassment of Human Rights Activist Narges Mohammadi', Gulf Centre for Human Rights, 14 November 2014, www.gc4hr.org/news/view/818 (accessed 27 April 2021).

During her time in prison, Narges was not able to communicate regularly with Kiana and Ali, her children who were now based in Paris.

In January 2019, to protest being denied access to medical care, Narges Mohammadi was reported to have begun a hunger strike, alongside the detained British-Iranian citizen Nazanin Zaghari-Ratcliffe, in Tehran's Evin Prison.

In December 2019, Narges and seven other feminist activists had staged a sit-in to express solidarity with the mourning families of the protestors killed in the November 2019 demonstrations. Prior to that, she had issued a public statement condemning the authorities for so many killings, the new wave of arrests and the maltreatment of new prisoners following the brutal November crackdown, during which the internet was also blocked by state authorities. It was later officially admitted that at least 304 people had been killed in three days, that hundreds had been injured and 7,000 arrested. However, independent sources such as Reuters reported that about 1,500 were killed. The Islamic Revolutionary Guard Corps were chiefly responsible for this crackdown.[5]

On 24 December 2019, in order to punish Narges Mohammadi for her activism inside Evin Prison in support of the November protesters, the authorities forcibly removed

5 Nayereh Tohidi, 'Iranian Feminist Narges Mohammadi is in Danger', *Ms.* magazine, 8 January 2020, msmagazine.com/2020/01/08/prominent-iranian-feminist-narges-mohammadi-is-in-danger (accessed 27 April 2021).

her from the facility and relocated her to a prison in the provincial city of Zanjan. There, Narges was deliberately placed alongside non-political prisoners, including drug dealers and smugglers, delinquents and violent criminals.

In early January 2020, Narges Mohammadi's mother, Ozra Bazargan, then able to visit her in Zanjan Prison, published a recorded appeal to international media and human rights organizations for help. Narges covertly released an open letter, illustrating both the cruelty of the prison authorities and her own bravery and resistance:

After four and a half months of deprivation from talking to my children on the phone, I am still in shock from the brutality and violence of the judiciary and security agents. After announcing our strike [the sit-down action in late December 2019 in Evin Prison], we witnessed the presence of a large number of security forces and intelligence agents alongside the prison authorities. The prison governor threatened that our action would not go without punishment, and our visiting hours and phone calls were canceled consequently.

On 24 December, I was shown a letter that my lawyer was in the prison to meet me. It turned out, it was a lie and there was no lawyer there. They took me to the prison governor's room, where he, in the presence of the agents from the Ministry of Intelligence, started shouting obscenities. I left the room and heard them running after me. He took my arms and wrenched them violently in order to stop me, and then they dragged me in the corridor.

While I was resisting, they bashed my hand to the door, and the smashed glass panel of the door cut my hands. My hands bleeding and wrenched, they threw me into an ambulance and started driving. But they stopped in front of ward 209. The prison governor said that he would not let me return to my ward and that he was sending me to the prison in Zanjan. I began chanting a song about Iran and they attacked, beat, and pushed me into a car to take me away. My hands were still bleeding, as the medicine I take for my medical condition does not let the blood clot, and the intelligence agents pressed the handcuffs hard on my wounds. The blood dripped on my clothes until we reached Zanjan. 24 December [2019] was the hideous day of the blatant brutality of the prison authorities and the security forces who have taken away all the means of life from me. What keeps me on my feet in this prison, while my body bruised and wounded, is my love for the honorable, but tormented, people of this country, and my ideals of justice and freedom. To honor the innocent people's blood shed atrociously, I pledge to speak the truth, defy tyranny, and defend the oppressed until my last breath.

Even after her release from prison in October 2020, Narges remained separated from her family. As refugees, her husband and children cannot travel back to Iran without getting arrested, and the government has refused to issue an exit visa for Narges. Moreover, only a few weeks after being released, Narges lost her mother to Covid-19 and then had to take care of her ailing father. But she was not granted a reprieve from the surveillance, threats and harassments by security agents.

None of these hardships have stopped Narges from her activism nor has she been less resilient than before. On 27 February 2021, Narges released a video via social media informing people that she had been summoned to court twice in December 2020, for a case that had been opened while she was still in prison. She announced that she has refused to appear in court and would not comply with any sentence passed. In the video, she described the sexual abuse and ill-treatment to which she and other women have been subjected in prisons, revealing that authorities have not yet responded to the complaint she made about this on 24 December 2020.

By this defiant action, Narges clarified to the public her position as the plaintiff, not the accused. She disclosed that the new case relates to the sit-in staged by her and other female political prisoners to protest the killing and arrests of protesters by security forces in November 2019, emphasising 'our protest in Evin entailed no violence and no wrong or illegal conduct.'

In March 2021, Narges wrote a foreword to the Iran Human Rights Annual Report on the Death Penalty in Iran. She stated that:

> The execution of people like Navid Afkari and Ruhollah Zam in the past year, have been the most ambiguous executions in Iran. Issuing the death penalty for Ahmadreza Djalali is one of the most erroneous sentences and the reasons for the issuance of these death sentences need to be carefully examined. These people have

been sentenced to death after being held in solitary confinement and subjected to horrific psychological and mental torture. That is why I do not consider the judicial process to be fair or just; I view keeping defendants in solitary confinement as a means to force them to make untrue and false confessions that are used as the key evidence in issuing such harsh sentences. That's why I am particularly worried about the recent arrests in Sistan and Baluchistan and Kurdistan, and I hope that anti-death penalty organizations will pay special attention to the detainees, because I fear that we will be facing another wave of executions over the coming year.

Since March 2021, Narges has initiated a new campaign to support political prisoners, focusing on the horrific impacts of solitary confinement or 'white torture' on the mental and physical wellbeing of prisoners.[6] As reported on the website of the DHRC on 21 April 2021, as of that day, seventeen prisoners of conscience in Evin and Rajai Shahr prisons have issued a petition protesting the illegal and inhumane practice of solitary confinement. They have recorded the duration of their incarceration in solitary confinement, while registering their complaints and demanding the prosecution of those responsible.

The report also refers to twenty-three former political prisoners who had experienced the horror of solitary

6 In assembling the timeline of these events, I drew upon the Wikipedia entry on Narges Mohammadi (en.wikipedia.org/wiki/Narges_Mohammadi#cite_note-ALF-5), corroborating the facts and dates with other sources, including Narges Mohammadi herself.

confinement and decided to register their complaint at the office of the Justice Ministry in Tehran. So far, forty complaints have been officially registered as a consequence of this new campaign led by Narges Mohammadi: the 'Unity Against Solitary Confinement'.[7]

The significance of Narges Mohammadi's role in Iran's civil rights and civil society

Narges Mohammadi is a seasoned, persistent and unifying model of civil rights activism. Her skills have been shaped through her extensive civic engagement in numerous organizations.

In the last twenty-eight years, Narges has been either a founder or an active member of eleven non-governmental organizations working toward codification of civil rights and human rights, including: the Student Association of Roushangaran (Enlightening Student Association) in the International University of Qazvin; the Enlightening Youth Association in the city of Qazvin; the Women's Association in Tehran; the Guild of Journalists in Tehran; the Association for Defence of the Rights of Prisoners; the Defenders of Human Rights Center; the National Council of Peace; the Committee for Defence of Free, Fair, and Safe Elections; the Stop Execution of the Child; LEGAM (the Campaign for

7 '17 Political Prisoners Join "Campaign of Unity Against Solitary Confinement"', Iran Human Rights, 22 April 2021, iranhr.net/en/articles/4709 (accessed 27 April 2021).

Step by Step Abolition of the Death Penalty); and the Center for Women's Citizenship. Furthermore, Narges Mohammadi's name (along with several prominent women's rights advocates such as Shirin Ebadi, Simin Behbahani and Shahla Lahidji) has been recorded as one of the initial supporters of the One Million Signatures Campaign to Change Discriminatory Laws, also known as the Change for Equality Campaign.[8]

In addition to national support among progressive Iranians inside and outside Iran, Narges Mohammadi has received several important international awards including: the 2018 Andrei Sakharov Prize from the American Physical Society, the 2016 Human Rights Award of the German city of Weimar and the 2011 Per Anger Prize, the Swedish government's international award for human rights. In 2010, when Nobel Laureate Shirin Ebadi won the Felix Ermacora Human Rights Award, she dedicated it to Narges Mohammadi, saying 'This courageous woman deserves this award more than I do.'

Narges is both respected and trusted across civil society and movements critical of the regime of the Islamic Republic because she is a uniter, not a divider. She has been helpful in converging progressive groups rather than splitting or polarizing them. She has avoided sectarianism and been energetic

8 Nayereh Tohidi, 'Iran's Women's Rights Movement and the One Million Signatures Campaign', *Change for Equality*, no. 208, November 2006/Azar 1385, www.we-change.org/spip.php?page=print&id_article=208 (accessed 27 April 2021).

in building coalitions spanning the full spectrum of political orientations, and supportive of diversity and pluralism. These are precious characteristics rarely present among many leading politicians in Iran's mainstream political culture.

In her own way, Narges is part of the growing counterculture in Iran that stands against the violent and ascetic culture preached by fanatic Islamist extremists: a life-affirming culture that embraces the pursuit of happiness, liberty and equality. Unlike the religious extremists among the current rulers who sacralize asceticism or hypocritically pretend in public to be ascetic, pious and strict 'men of god', but behave immorally in private, Narges is among those who believe we should honestly and openly promote beauty, happiness, non-violence and joy.

Nayereh Tohidi
April 2021

INTRODUCTION: IN SOLIDARITY

This book is an important collection of interviews conducted by Narges Mohammadi with women who were (and are) incarcerated for holding religious, ethical and political beliefs that do not conform to the repressive conditions of the Islamic Republic of Iran. In this volume, Narges and thirteen other women document, narrate and discuss a specific form of torture being used against them in the carceral context at the heart of contemporary Iranian society: extreme sensory deprivation, known as white torture. Those who document white torture in this book are Narges Mohammadi, Nigara Afsharzadeh, Sima Kiani, Sedigheh Moradi, Atena Daemi, Mahvash Shahriari, Zahra Zahtabchi, Hengameh Shahidi, Reyhaneh Tabatabaei, Fatemeh (Mary) Mohammadi, Nazila Nouri, Nazanin Zaghari-Ratcliffe, Shokoufeh Yadollahi and Marzieh Amiri Ghahfarrokhi.

This short introduction contextualizes these interviews, which form the first book-length analysis of how the Islamic regime in Iran widely uses white torture. This book consists entirely of the testimonies of those women who have experienced it, and are experiencing it still in some cases, while being incarcerated for political reasons. This work provides the most detailed documentation so far of how the regime specifically targets and tortures women accused of political offences against the state.[1] Mohammadi has drawn together so many voices and experiences in this collection that the already flourishing field of Iranian women's prison memoirs is greatly enriched by information about what is happening in 2020 in Iran.[2] The hard work and courage of the women who have shared their experiences and knowledge in this collection is powerful, painful and demands action.

White Torture unveils how the Islamic Republic of Iran demands the total annihilation of a belief in justice, and how it tortures women for advocating human rights, for their religion or, in cases like Nazanin Zaghari-Ratcliffe's, in order to pressure other states to negotiate with Iran. From

---

1 For a study of the torture and conditions of women incarcerated as so-called 'regular' prisoners, as distinct from political prisoners, see Nahid Rahimipour Anaraki, *Prison in Iran: A Known Unknown*, Palgrave Macmillan, 2021.

2 Notable women's memoirs of surviving torture as political prisoners in Iran in English include Olya Roohizadegan, *Olya's Story: A Survivor's Personal and Dramatic Account of the Persecution of Baha'is in Revolutionary Iran*, Oneworld Publications, 1993; Azadeh Agah, Sousan Mehr, Shadi Parsi and Shahrzad Mojab, *We Lived to Tell: Political Prison Memoirs of Iranian Women*, McGilligan Books, 2007; Marina Nemat, *Prisoner of Tehran*, Free Press, 2008; Zarah Ghahramani, *My Life as a Traitor*, Scribe, 2008; Shahla Talebi, *Ghosts of Revolution: Rekindled Memories of Imprisonment in Iran*, Stanford University Press, 2011; 'Sepideh's Diary: A Shocking Glimpse into Women's Prisons in Iran', *IranWire*, 29 July 2020, iranwire.com/en/features/7382 (accessed 27 April 2021).

its very beginning, the Islamic regime has taken hostages in order to exert pressure on the prisoner's family and community and to terrorize society into submission. These testimonies show that white torture inflicts deep wounds, but also that it cannot achieve what the regime intends. The Islamic regime cannot separate a woman from her love for her family, her fellow citizens, or her God. This book introduces us to a group of women who clearly speak with all their senses and their soul; they are the antidote to white torture: they build strength, solidarity and love.

Torture is not new in Iranian society or prisons. Scholars such as Darius M. Rejali and Ervand Abrahamian have documented how men in Iran have used a wide range of torture methods against those they incarcerated throughout the last century.[3] (It should also be noted that the governments of the United States of America, the United Kingdom and myriad other states have also relied on torture within prisons to control.[4]) The Iranian regime, which is currently clinging to power at great cost to the people, came to power in 1979 after two years of popular revolt against the ruling Pahlavi dynasty. Though the Islamic regime assumed

3 Darius M. Rejali, *Torture And Modernity: Self, Society, And State In Modern Iran*, Westview Press, 1994; Ervand Abrahamian, *Tortured Confessions: Prisons and Public Recantations in Modern Iran*, University of California Press, 1999.

4 W. Fitzhugh Brundage, *Civilizing Torture: An American Tradition*, Belknap, 2018; Frank Foley, 'The (de)legitimation of torture: rhetoric, shaming and narrative contestation in two British cases', *European Journal of International Relations*, vol. 27, no. 1, 2021, 102–6, available online at doi.org/10.1177/1354066120950011 (accessed 1 April 2022).

government with promises to end the Shah's use of an extensive intelligence system, corrupt judiciary and widespread torture for social control, they have instead fortified these institutions to control society, refusing to tolerate any dissent. Since 1979 the regime has consistently targeted individuals for their political beliefs (communists, leftists, unionists and others) and adherents of religions other than Shi'a Islam. The state has institutionally and socially excluded Bahá'í s, Christians and dervishes, and has used the prison system, including torture and interrogation, in an attempt to force prisoners to recant publicly their beliefs and actions.[5]

The Islamic regime has used legislation and physical coercion to create a society in which women and ethnic and religious minorities have restricted rights of movement, education and employment. Individuals who politically organize, protest or speak against the state are flogged, imprisoned and executed. As you will see, the Iranian state targets and persecutes families across generations, threatening to incarcerate and torture political prisoners' children – and sometimes doing so – to further push families into total socio-economic exclusion and isolation. The Islamic Republic of Iran is a carceral state: the intense cruelty and torture in prisons dictates a lesson to the world at large.

This is unacceptable.

Peaceful resistance to the regime has been unrelenting and continues to grow. Human rights groups and families protest

5 See Abrahamian, *Tortured Confessions*, 1999.

the secret, public and mass executions, and incarceration, that the regime perpetrates with or without due process.[6] In 2020, the Covid-19 pandemic inflicted disastrous consequences because medical aid has been crippled by the state's secrecy, lack of investment in healthcare and by international sanctions. In 2020, the number of citizens or activists incarcerated by the state has increased by 35 per cent, the convictions of religious minorities increased by 28.9 per cent, convictions against freedom of expression have increased by 52.9 per cent and convictions against unions have increased by 89 per cent.[7] Since the 1990s, the Iranian regime has changed its torture techniques because of their refusal to accept even the existence of individuals whose religious or ethical or political beliefs don't conform to the state's. Instead of injuring prisoners in order to elicit information valuable to the state, the Islamic state relies on attacking human consciousness.[8] White torture lies at the core of torture in the

6 For example, 'On 1 March, 2021, a group of civil rights activists appeared before the Judiciary Services Office in Tehran to file a suit against those who order or enforce solitary confinement in Iran's detention centres and prisons, bringing to the fore public discussion in Iran of a longstanding practice that the UN has labelled torture.' Reported in 'Lawsuit by Civil Rights Activists Reignites Debate on Solitary Confinement in Iran's Prisons', Center for Human Rights in Iran, 11 March 2021, www.iranhumanrights.org/2021/03/lawsuit-by-civil-rights-activists-reignites-debate-on-solitary-confinement-in-irans-prisons (accessed 1 April 2022).
7 'HRA Annual Statistical Report of Human Rights Conditions in Iran – 2020', Human Rights Activists News Agency, p. 42, www.en-hrana.org/wp-content/uploads/2020/12/Hrana-Annual-Report-2020-EN.pdf (accessed 1 April 2022).
8 Rejali, *Torture and Modernity*, p. 11.

carceral complex, pervasively used alongside confinement and isolation for political prisoners. The aim of white torture is to permanently break the connection between a person's body and mind in order to force the individual to recant their ethics and actions.

What is white torture?

The authors of this book comprehensively describe and analyse the torture of sensory deprivation as it is practised in Iran. White torture deprives prisoners of all sensory stimulation over long periods, and this is applied to prisoners of conscience and political prisoners, alongside the techniques of solitary confinement and interrogation. The state often incarcerates people outside the formal judiciary system, meaning that they are in prison without trial, and the victim therefore is aware that there is no impartial court to which they can appeal. Incarceration without trial is used as a weapon of torture and oppression in Iran. Indeed, in 2020 alone 147 prisoners made reports to Human Rights Activists in Iran about being kept 'in an unsure state about their sentence and situation'.[9]

White torture is inflicted through the architecture of the prison, the conduct of the staff and the interrogators' questions. The control of light in the cell removes the body's

9　'HRA Annual Statistical Report of Human Rights Conditions in Iran – 2020', p. 36.

ability to know night from day and disrupts sleeping patterns. Prisoners are blindfolded when they leave the cell. The lack of touch in solitary confinement and in interrogation causes pain, and this is compounded by being able to feel only the cell's concrete floor and walls and coarse blankets. The only smell in the cell is often a filthy toilet kept in that state precisely to assault the prisoner's olfactory sense. The food provided to prisoners is bland, unchanging and served at room temperature in a metal bowl, and tea is given in a plastic cup. The following chapters describe the effects of these measures.

Narges shows us how even when the prisoner can understand that they are being subjected to white torture – and that it is designed to cause fear – sensory deprivation nonetheless results in physiological effects such as anxiety. As documented here, white torture radically disorients and destabilizes the body, inducing anguish as well as neurological and cardiac conditions. Many university psychology departments across the USA conducted experiments in this field through the 1950s and 1960s, and it has been shown that sensory deprivation causes 'complicated hallucinations, deterioration in intellectual and perceptual functions, and a greater susceptibility to propaganda'.[10] It is for this reason that the Islamic regime has institutionalized the use of white torture alongside beatings, interrogation and solitary confinement.

10 John P. Zubek, *Sensory Deprivation: Fifteen Years of Research*, Appleton-Century, 1969.

As with other forms of torture, white torture is designed to cause damage that continues beyond prison.[11] People subjected to white torture suffer from ongoing medical conditions, and from the knowledge that human beings can perform such barbaric acts. 'White torture causes one to remain in a state of distrust of everyone and everything. Victims' words are not trusted by people on the outside, either. This leads people to feel pushed into isolation, as the regime intends.'[12] The sensory deprivation of white torture physiologically tethers sensory stimulation to the traumatic experience so that sounds, tastes and experiences in the outside world reinvoke the pain of prison.

Amir Rezanezhad, who has translated this book and worked with me on this introduction, describes the effects of white torture on the prisoner after release. 'You wish to be with your family and friends but can't stand being with them. Silence agonizes you. Any voice or sound agonizes you all the same. Anxiety is always in the background of your life and deprives you of sleep. You see yourself and the interrogator in your nightmares, either in solitary confinement, interrogation rooms or even in the place where you live, wherever it is.'[13]

People who have been imprisoned know that they can be detained again at any time. This is intentional torture. White

---

11　See Elaine Scarry, *The Body in Pain: The Making and Unmaking of the World*, Oxford University Press, 1988.

12　Amir Rezanezhad, 'Reflections on the effects of incarceration and torture', unpublished manuscript, 2021.

13　Rezanezhad, op. cit.

torture is easy for the regime to apply and its impact is striking and painful. When Narges was incarcerated on charges of conspiracy to disrupt national security, she stated that 'the only way to get out of the cell was confession, repentance and cooperation.' The regime is not attempting to extract information, but to control people, especially women, by making it clear that their religious, ethical or political beliefs are a threat that the state will go to any extremes to eliminate.

The effects of persecution, incarceration and torture on women are different to the effects on men. Women are more vulnerable than men to the socio-economic effects of isolation due to the heavily policed and unique status of women in the labour market and society. Women are also more vulnerable to torture in incarceration than men due to their roles as mothers and carers in their families.[14] This is not to say that men do not suffer from the knowledge that their families will also be persecuted when they are imprisoned, or that men do not suffer from separation from their children. All prisoners suffer due to their isolation from those they love and who love them.

Due to women's social position in Iranian society, they are tortured as the primary carers of their children. Interrogators accuse them of bringing harm to their children through their supposedly shameful beliefs, and of

14 See Shahed Alavi, 'Shocking Stories of Abuse, Harassment and Humiliation of Female Prisoners in Iran', *IranWire*, 25 January 2020, iranwire.com/en/features/6654 (accessed 1 April 2022).

course these women have reckoned with this cost prior to their imprisonment. Interrogators work on prisoners to aggravate these wounds with the direct invocation of social shame and stigma. The regime also victimizes mothers in prison by refusing them contact with their children as a form of torture. As Rahimipour Anaraki concludes in her 2019 study of the prison system in Iran, 'women prisoners are controlled by the penitentiary administration through their children.'[15]

Narges knew that her interrogators had all the information they needed about her work, but they often used interrogations to accuse her of failing and harming her children. The interrogators demanded that she resign from her role with the Defenders of Human Rights Center. She refused, and they continued to subject her to white torture and also removed her weekly call to her family, to coerce her into capitulating.[16] This book shows the strength of the women who continue to demand both their right to speak out for justice and their right to raise their children. The Islamic regime uses violent torture to maintain its hold on power – it acts immorally by any standard.

Through these fourteen accounts of white torture, we learn the extent of the measures taken in the carceral system

15 Rahimipour Anaraki, *Prison in Iran*, p. 167.
16 Narges Mohammadi has spoken out about the regime's use of children in the torture of mothers – see, for example, 'Shocking report about mothers in prison in Iran', *Iran Focus*, 10 February 2017, www.iranfocus.com/en/women/31243-shocking-report-about-mothers-in-prison-in-iran (accessed 2 April 2022).

to silence women. These individual experiences provide valuable insight into the statistics published about incarceration and the persecution of minorities in Iran today.

The women featured in this book are either currently incarcerated or recently released and facing new charges. They have put their experiences of intense torture into words within the prison itself. This is an awesome feat, uniting voice, intellect and emotion to analyse and testify to a form of torture that aims to destroy the capacity to do exactly this. As the contributors have not been able to edit or review their accounts, Amir Rezanezhad has honoured their work with a literal translation. These words should be read keeping in mind the intensity of pressure on the authors, and paying close attention to the details. When authors repeat certain details multiple times throughout their work, this repetition articulates the importance of these details and the trauma inflicted by them, as Rezanezhad has observed.[17] His translation pays both ethical and intellectual homage to the unique power of these women to speak out against silence.

The traumatic impact of white torture cannot be exaggerated. Women contributed to this volume even as Islamic regime judges, intelligence agents and guards tortured them. This makes it an outstanding and important contribution to scholarship.

The authors of this book record the cruelty of white torture and the strength they have had to find to live through it.

17 Rezanezhad, op. cit.

These are the words of people who understand the fears and weaknesses of the regime better than the regime itself, and they document how the tools of torture fail to separate them from their humanity and their belief in justice and love. This volume speaks truth to power, against the full force of the state. These women document the way the Iranian state tries to separate their souls from their bodies through white torture, and in doing so they build something bigger and more powerful than individual survival – they build networks of solidarity.

Shannon Woodcock

INTERVIEWS AND
TESTIMONIES

NARGES MOHAMMADI

My husband, Taghi Rahmani, was arrested alongside members of the Council of Nationalist-Religious Activists and members of the Freedom Movement. Following these arrests, on 19 March 2001 we, the families of those arrested, protested against the illegal actions of the Islamic Revolutionary Guard Corps (IRGC) and the judiciary. Part of our activism included rallies in front of the judiciary, parliament and the UN office. We also conducted internal and external interviews referring to the responsible institutions. This is why Branch 26 of the Revolutionary Court headed by Hassan Zare – Haddad – summoned me.[1] An interrogator from the IRGC came. In one of the rooms of the Revolutionary Court he asked me a few questions about my interview, which was published in the newspaper he had brought with him.

1 Hassan Zare Dehnavi, known as Judge Haddad, was the deputy security director of the Tehran Public and Revolutionary Prosecutor's Office. He was accused of numerous human rights violations and was known for his cruel treatment of prisoners. He died in October 2020.

He then took me to Branch 26, where I was arrested. I was arrested on the orders of the interrogator in charge of the office even though the judge had not yet come to the branch. The branch called the judge to come to the office to sign my arrest warrant. I waited for about an hour for the judge to come, and when he arrived he signed the form without even saying a word or asking me a question. Then the interrogator took me out.

We left through the back door of the Revolutionary Court and got in a Peugeot car. I was told to lower my head and they blindfolded me. We then drove through several streets before entering a different building through a large door. We left and then travelled a long distance in the car. Outside, the streets were very quiet. I got out, still blindfolded, and went in. I felt like we were inside a remote castle. I was taken to a prison ward and then to a small solitary cell.

It was the first time I'd been locked in a cell. What a strange environment; a small box without a window or the slightest way out. A very small skylight, up above my head, but almost no natural light entered. High up, in a hole in the wall, a small 100-watt light bulb that never went out.

I had heard that a projector with a powerful light had been on day and night in Hoda Saber's[2] cell. I had heard that cells were about the size of a human being with outstretched hands. I had heard that pure silence reigned in the prison

2 Hoda Saber was an Iranian intellectual and activist who went on hunger strike in 2011 in Evin Prison, and died of a heart attack soon afterwards.

and that the door opened and closed three to four times a day for going to the toilet and performing ablutions for prayer. I went over what I had heard about solitary confinement's function: white torture and brainwashing. Now I was experiencing what I had heard and read about, and I knew the terrible consequences it could inflict. I was suddenly afraid.

I didn't know where I was or what they would do to me. The unknown punishments in the prison and the uncertainty of the future were like a deadly poison. I wondered how it was possible to treat a human being like that. What happens to the right to breathe, to walk, to go to the bathroom freely, to hear the voices of other people and talk to them? Being deprived of the most basic rights frightened me more than thinking about the charges, the trial and the conviction.

I sat in the cell for hours until a man opened the door and said, 'Come out.' Before I went out, I put on my coat, scarf and blindfold. In the hallway I noticed I was in a men's ward. At the behest of the jailer, I had clumsily blindfolded myself so tightly that I could not see and it was difficult for me to walk. A man walked in front of me and guided me.

A little further on I supposed that I passed a door, and he guided me back to the right. I turned back and hit the wall. I heard two men laughing behind me and I was very upset. They took me into a small room, took some pictures and then ordered me to put the blindfold back on. I was sent back to the cell. It was like a physical ache, the disturbing sound of door locks opening and closing. They had given me coloured paper to put out under the door when I needed to go to the bathroom. The jailer came. I said I wanted to go to the toilet. He told me to put the blindfold on. 'No,' I said, 'because what happened in the hallway was insulting and you laughed at me.' He closed the door and left. I put the paper out several times and he came, but because I was not blindfolded he closed the door and left. So, when I started shouting, one of them, who was very violent, ordered me to stand behind the door when I was inside the cell so that I would not see them. I stood up and started talking. He was apparently one of the ward officials. I explained what had happened and why I would not put the blindfold on.

They brought a radio and turned it up so that people in the other cells couldn't hear us. They were incredibly careful not to be heard by the nearby cells in the ward. Finally, he ordered me to pull my scarf down to my chin and keep my head down and go to the bathroom. A jailer followed me along the corridor. In the last cell before the toilet, I noticed that the prisoners were all men – it was the men's ward.

Later I found out that Dr Baniasadi, Dr Gharavi, Mr Tavassoli, Mr Sabbaghian and other members of the Freedom Movement of Iran were kept in nearby cells. I went to the toilet, which seemed unhygienic. I came out. I heard the voice of a jailer standing just a few steps away from the toilet. I protested that he should stand a little further away. He said that it was not my business where he stood and that I had to relieve myself, regardless. He told me to wash my hands in the basin. The Golnar soap was disintegrated and watery when I picked it up.[3] Then I returned to the cell. I was not allowed to say a word in the hallway.

When it was my turn to take a bath, a male prison guard came and gave me some shampoo and said I could take a shower. As when they took me to the toilet, he came and stood a few steps behind me. I entered the bathroom with trepidation. How dirty the bathroom looked! But I had no alternative. I stood in the middle of the bathroom and shower to avoid touching anything. I did not even dare to close my eyes to wash my hair under the shower. There was no lock in the bathroom. I had closed the door. I blinked and made sure no one came in. I did not feel safe at all. My arguments with the guards to get them further away from the toilet and bathroom were useless and I had to put up with the situation. One day, looking at the corridor of the ward through the narrow gap in the cell, I saw an old man who was accompanied and given personal care by someone. The old man had put a towel on his head. The heat was terrible. It was September 2001. I noticed that he didn't feel well due to the heat and was taken out. The man was Taher Ahmadzadeh,[4] accompanied by Mr Na'impour.[5] It was only after my release that I recalled this moment and learned his identity.

3 A rather old and common brand of soap in Iran.
4 Taher Ahmadzadeh Heravi (1921–2017) was the first governor of Khorasan after the 1979 Revolution, and a key figure of the Freedom Movement.
5 A member of the Freedom Movement of Iran.

At Ishratabad Military Detention Centre, the guards, prisoners, staff and doctors were all men and I was the only woman in the cell. I remembered that Firoozeh Saber[6] had described a similar situation before me and that she had been imprisoned there. She'd said that she had seen Mr Rajaei[7] there, so she'd probably been imprisoned in the same ward. Days and nights would not pass for me. Time stood still. I did not have a watch. I guessed the time from the call to prayer, which was played three times a day. The cell was only three steps in width and walking backwards and forwards made me dizzy, but I had to put up with it. When I sat for a long time, I felt the walls close in on me. At night I sang songs and practised the lessons that I had learned in singing class before going to sleep, but every time the jailer would open the door and tell me not to sing. So I had to whisper. I hadn't heard anyone's voice for a long time so when I raised my voice a little I was surprised. Once I was praying without wearing a headscarf and coat, and the prison guard opened the door. Although he saw me praying, he paused for a while and then called me for interrogation. When I was being taken for questioning, the jailer would roll up a newspaper, putting one end in my hand and the other end in his own hand.

There were small cells in the area where the interrogation took place, from which I sometimes heard the voices of men.

6 Hoda Saber's sister.
7 Alireza Rajaei is an Iranian journalist and part of the religious opposition to the current regime.

I was once in an interrogation cell when Taghi was sent in as well. Taghi looked surprised and a little nervous. We didn't have much time. He said a few short sentences and advised me to exercise, and then he was taken out again. I was interrogated at night as well.

Once it was so late that I was interrogated in my cell. When they called my interrogator out of the cell, he left and another man came in and told me to turn my chair around. When I did so, I saw Judge Haddad. He sat down in front of me and talked about his concern for the prisoners and his efforts to save their lives. I'd felt sick that morning and they'd taken me to Baqiyatallah Hospital. He asked me if I could sleep at night. 'I sleep, but not well,' I said, 'the cell upsets me. I put a blanket under my head and spread a blanket under it, but the blanket badly hurts my face and body.'

He talked for a while and left, and the interrogator returned to the cell and continued where he had left off. It was hot in the cell and I couldn't breathe easily, so I couldn't exercise. I had no appetite. I would take the food but give it back untouched. I repeatedly asked the jailer to leave the corner of the door open. I was sick of the door being always closed. Later, talking to a psychiatrist, I realized that I had claustrophobia.

Being in the cell was hard and sometimes unbearable. I yearned to have a heart attack, just to get out of there. Because I really did not know what they wanted from me as they didn't ask me about my activities and there was no ongoing investigation. They threatened me all the time. They said Taghi was going to be executed, or that he would be imprisoned for a long time. 'Taghi won't come back,' the interrogator once said. 'Look out for yourself.' I just remember how bad it was to hear that. I cried. My tears flowed and I tried my best not to cry there and then. I was facing the wall and the interrogator was right behind me in that very small cell. I remember the interrogator pressing the tip of his pen against my shoulder several times while I was talking, and I was very surprised.

I touched my bare feet in the slippers, which were twice the normal size. They were frozen. The interrogator noticed that I was not feeling well. It was night and I had not eaten dinner. He gave me a glass of mint syrup and I was so sick that I drank it up.

When the interrogators saw fit, I was taken out for fresh air, but there was no routine in place at all. The food was served in a stainless steel or aluminium bowl. For water they gave me an old plastic cup. They offered nothing but three meals of breakfast, lunch and dinner. The food was poor and I couldn't eat well. Sitting in the cell, I felt that the world had stopped. I was anxious and scared. I can't say I was sad or depressed, but I didn't feel like a normal human being.

Second experience, June 2010

Ali and Kiana were three and a half years old. Kiana had recently had surgery. We went to the hospital to examine her wounds on both sides of her abdomen and returned home at about ten o'clock at night. I was hurrying to get the kids ready to put them to sleep when the doorbell rang. Officers were standing in the yard. Some of them came up and started searching the house. It was time for the children to go to bed, but they were crying. Ali used to sleep on my feet. I put him on my feet, and he fell asleep. I hugged Kiana. She had a fever and no matter what I did, she wouldn't sleep. She was restless. Clasping her hands around my neck, she looked at the men ploughing through the house.

It was time for me to leave. Separation from Kiana was one of the hardest and most heartrending events of my life. Kiana cried in Taghi's arms, 'Mum, don't go.' The officers were standing on the steps, ordering me to hurry up and move. I had come halfway down the stairs when Kiana said in a thin, sick voice, crying, 'Mum, come and kiss me.' I looked at the officer. 'Go!' he said. I ran up the stairs. I kissed her firmly. She had a fever, and I was burning from the pain of being separated from her. I came down the stairs, feeling inert and powerless. I prayed I wouldn't tremble. The door was closed, and I left my heart back inside, before I got in the car.

It was midnight. The city was quiet. The car in front and the car I was in sped all the way to Evin. The heavy iron prison gate opened, and I was handed directly to the Ministry of Intelligence. They blindfolded me immediately. A heavy, dirty curtain was hanging in front of the doorway, which they pulled aside. I entered. The female prison guard admitted me and took me to a cell. She ordered me to strip naked. 'What do you mean?' I asked her. 'Even underwear?' She said yes. I had a row with her, but she was a relatively violent woman and of course familiar with the process, and unfortunately she succeeded in getting what she wanted, not paying any attention to my discomfort.

From the moment I entered prison, I was shocked by this shameful act and by the arrogance and audacity of these women. I couldn't believe that they were not even ashamed of doing these things. They acted as if they had done something brilliant. They gave me a uniform of crimson plastic cloth that looked like a coat and trousers and told me to wear it. I said I wanted comfortable clothes. They said that this was my dress. They gave me a black headscarf with white flowers and told me to cover my hair. They also gave me a blindfold and ordered me to cover my eyes, and a chador to put over my head, then they took me straight to the interrogation room. There were two men in the room; one was sitting at a table in front of me and one behind me. They started asking irrelevant and endless questions that I refused to answer because I had not yet been arraigned.

The interrogator behind me began to accuse me of immoral conduct. He started talking about irrelevant things such as the insecurity of society, even public places like parks, and the existence of prostitutes, and then he got to the members of Defenders of Human Rights Center and my actions. When he started talking about me, I became so angry that I lost control. I got up, turned around, and faced him. Weren't they ashamed? I protested. Of arresting a woman at her home, separating her from her two young children, in the presence of her husband, in the middle of the night, and interrogating and slandering her?

I'd raised my voice. He, too, started shouting and threatening. He said that I would be sentenced to at least one year in prison for what I did. I picked up an A4 sheet from the interrogator's desk and started writing a complaint. He went out and returned a few minutes later with a complaint form against me for getting up, turning around and seeing the interrogator's face. The other interrogator began to say I had espionage allegations against me for affiliation with US and British intelligence agencies. I protested that before I had even been arraigned, they were accusing me of all sorts of things and even asking written questions accordingly. 'Don't I need to know my accusation first?' I said. 'To see if I have to answer these questions?' The argument lasted for hours and I was finally sent back to my cell.

The cell was larger than the one in Ishratabad. The ceiling and the concrete walls were painted cream. It was a lifeless space. There was a very old carpet on the floor with three military blankets. I made a 'bed': a blanket underneath my body, a blanket under my head and a blanket pulled over me, and slept. In the morning I was given a plastic cup of tea, a piece of cheese and some bread. Then they took me for interrogation. I constantly protested that what they were doing was illegal because I had not yet been informed of the charges.

Finally, I was taken to Mr Kianmanesh[8] in the Ardabili Court. I explained that about a month before, on the same charge of propaganda against the regime, I had been released on bail in Branch 4 of the Revolutionary Court by the order of Mr Jamali. Mr Kianmanesh told me to write the same to the prosecutor. I wrote and asked for this illegal detention to be investigated because I had been rearrested on a charge I had already been tried for, and he promised to investigate. I was sent back to the cell. That is, despite the fact that the interrogator knew about the incident, I was detained, and the interrogations continued.

My experience in solitary confinement in 2010 was significantly different from my experience in solitary confinement in 2001 because this time I was a mother. My children were very young. I fed them, put them to sleep, calmed them down, bathed them, told stories for them and played games with them. And now suddenly all this was taken from me. It was as if I were no longer me. Could I have imagined and endured the removal of Ali and Kiana from my arms before this? It was as if I had lost everything, even my hands and feet.

Interrogation conditions were difficult because the only way to get out of the cell was confession, repentance and

8 The deputy and advisor to the head of the Prisons Organization at the time.

cooperation. They called me again and took me to court. This time I wasn't taken to Mr Kianmanesh, who had not issued an arrest warrant for me, but to Mr Mohebbi, who used a legal trick and a new charge of conspiracy to disrupt national security as an excuse to keep me in my cell. He had dug out this charge days after my detention. I asked him on what grounds they had accused me.

'Why weren't these accusations made on the first day?' I asked. 'Why didn't Mr Kianmanesh make these accusations?' But he replied that he didn't know about Mr Kianmanesh. That was how he acted. I was sent back to the cell. The cell did not have enough light. A weak light was on that never went out. The window was very high up and just below the ceiling, but behind it there was a thick iron grille. This prevented me from seeing the sky and it let only a little light through. The windows were closed and not the slightest fresh air flowed in. I was in the second hallway. My cell number was 24. The silence was deathly. The absence of light, air, smell and sound seclude the prisoner from natural living conditions. I have always thought that the conditions of a cell do not differ from the conditions of a human being in a can.

The cell door was locked from the other side. The iron hatch on the cell was locked from the outside. The window was locked from the outside and never opened. Everything was locked. The air was behind the lock. The light was behind the lock. The sound was behind the lock and the prisoner had no power to break the locks. I was afraid of

the enclosed environment and whatever arguments I
made to myself, rationalizing that the locked door and
window didn't pose any dangers and I didn't have to be
afraid, they did not work for me. Anxiety overwhelmed
me.

The interrogators and staff who worked on the ward or
came to meet their defendants rang the bell to pick them up
and take them for interrogation. The bell sounded like an
old bell in a residential house. You can't imagine how the
sound tore my heart. The footsteps of the woman jailer
began: tick tock tick. If she stood in front of my cell door, I
was horrified that I was being interrogated. If she passed
my cell, I would worry about why I was left in the cell and
how long I would stay. When I was released from prison, I
heard this sound over and over again in my sleep and
waking hours, and anxiety ran through my veins and made
me recoil.

There was fresh air time every other day. I was allowed to
walk in the yard for two minutes in a coat, scarf and slippers.
The courtyard was lifeless, engulfed by high walls and a ceiling with iron bars, bereft of plants or trees. The bath was
every other day. Going to the toilet was limited to certain
times. If you lit the signals for going to the toilet more than
you were supposed to, the guards responded with aggression. The prison guards deliberately avoided talking to the
prisoners, even greeting them. It was assumed to be natural
that a prisoner had to be deprived of all human interaction
and kept in a cell.

I remember one night, in my sleep, I felt Kiana's lips on my cheek with the warmth I had always experienced, and this feeling was quite palpable and real. Kiana was leaning towards me. It was so real that I would never call it a dream. Kiana was in the cell next to me. When I opened my arms to hug her, I fell into a void. My eyes were open, my hands reached out for her and I was back in the cell. Kiana was not there, and I cried so bitterly that night that I will never forget those tears.

One day they gave me an orange. I ate only a few slices of the orange each day so that it would not run out too soon. I kept its skin and sculpted it into the shape of the earth. Kiana means the essence and soul of nature and this orange was the essence of life for me. I walked around it and prayed for Kiana, still recovering from surgery. I often said during interrogations that I missed Ali and Kiana, but it had no effect on the interrogators.

One day I was taken about two floors down from the ward in the elevator. The interrogator said, 'Master has come.' I entered a room with a video camera and stands and projectors. I was surprised. There was a middle-aged, tall man in a suit in the room who I would never have imagined was an interrogator if I had seen him outside. Of course, I think he was really the master of interrogation. His expression was icy and unmoved. When I told him that my children were small and that I was a mother, he said, 'Are not the mothers of Gaza mothers?' This statement revealed what kind of person he was and I realized that no issues could be discussed with him. He spoke incessantly and considered people like Bazargan[9] and Sahabi[10] and all the intellectual movements to be eclectic and non-Muslim. When I came out of the room, I felt that I had been drained of energy and I could not even walk. I remembered a sentence I had heard that some of the interrogators had been trained to drain the prisoner's energy and put psychological pressure on them.

They didn't investigate my activities in the Human Rights Defenders Center, the National Peace Council, in the Committee for the Protection of Votes, or campaigning against the execution of underage children, even though these activities were the reasons for the charge of 'acting against national security'.

There was not the slightest question about my interviews, as I was accused of 'propaganda against the regime'. From the first night they had put forward a baseless hypothesis that they maintained until the day I was released: claiming without any documentary evidence that the Defenders of Human Rights Center was established by the western intelligence services through Ms Ebadi, and that we were the agents of those services. They had strange requests. There was no preliminary research at all. One day during the interrogations they insisted that I had to announce the dissolution of

9 Mehdi Bazargan was the first prime minister of Iran after the 1979 Revolution. He resigned his position in the same year to protest the siege of the US embassy in Tehran.
10 Ezzatollah Sahabi was an Iranian politician and journalist and a leader of Iran's Nationalist-Religious movement, an opposition group.

the Center in a written statement, which I refused to do. Then they moved on to another proposal. This time I was asked to resign from the position of vice president of DHRC. They had even planned it. 'We will bring Soltani, Seifzadeh and Dadkhah,' the interrogator said.[11] 'You just say in their presence that you will no longer be the vice president of the Center.' I declined again.

Once they told me to announce publicly that we'd stop our cooperation with Ms Ebadi. Earlier in the year, during interrogations in Suhrawardi, interrogators insisted that I stopped working with Ms Ebadi. They promised that in place of that cooperation, the Ministry of Intelligence would provide many facilities, including an office and permission to travel abroad, attend and hold seminars and meetings on human rights with guests from other countries. I refused.

Finally, in their last attempts, they tried to make me write a letter of repentance and remorse. One night the interrogator called me to the interrogation room. 'Get ready for tomorrow,' he said, 'you must express your remorse for your activities in front of the camera and announce your resignation to the members of the Center.' I said that I wouldn't. When I returned to my cell, my whole body was drenched with sweat. I really tried to be calm in these conflicts and confrontations, but no matter how much I tried, it was

11 Abdolfattah Soltani, Mohammad Seifzadeh and Seyed Mohammad Ali Dadkhah are co-founders of the Defenders of Human Rights Center.

hard to bear what they were trying to impose on me. I felt that morality had been forgotten and humanity had collapsed at the prison threshold. Interrogators don't want to know about your true self. They want to build a new person moulded in their image. I was sure that the interrogator did not consider me a spy or a traitor, but the fact that he asked me to write a letter of repentance by accepting the Center's affiliation with western security institutions distressed me.

One of my interrogators once tried to reprimand me for my housekeeping. 'Are you not ashamed?' he said. 'You are an engineering inspector. Your spouse is a writer. I saw the state of your house on the night we went there. I'm asking you, why do you live in such conditions? Do you deserve that house and furniture?' I was scolded and condemned by the interrogators for any and every reason, and the interrogators always behaved this way when talking to me about Ali and Kiana.

When a human being is in this situation, they are pushed to the brink of impatience, restlessness, anxiety and madness due to the disrupted living conditions and being deprived of basic human needs. Imagine how destructive it would be to be scolded and belittled because your children are without their mother – the price they constantly make you pay for your activism.

As a mother, I missed Ali and Kiana relentlessly and because of this, they would connect part of the interrogations to news about them. For example, one day an interrogator came and said 'they have taken your children from your house'. I got up, 'Where to?' I asked. 'They were taken from Tehran to Qazvin to your mother-in-law's.'

At that moment I felt heartbroken that Ali and Kiana weren't asleep in their own beds and were not in the room they were used to, leaving behind their toys. Tears welled up in my eyes. The interrogator left me there. I was sitting on a chair. I was very ill. I saw that I was alone in the cell and they were gone. I stood up to pray without a mat and with an unbearable headache, and God witnessed these difficult moments of mine.

It was the eighth day of my detention. I was returned to my own cell after a lengthy interrogation. My hands were numb. My legs also became a little numb and immobile. I thought it was better to inform the prison guard before I became worse. The jailer came and I explained that I was a little sick. He went and came back and said 'Put on your chador and go to the hospital.'

There is a room in Ward 4 with two beds, an ECG machine and some medical supplies. If a prisoner feels unwell or something happens to them, they will be taken there to see the doctor. I got up, put on my chador and set off. I hadn't walked more than a few steps in the corridor when, I don't know how, but I hit the ground hard. I was a little dizzy and heavy, but I hadn't fainted. My legs were completely weak and numb. I felt paralysed. My tongue did not move in my mouth. I couldn't speak. My voice trailed off and was incomprehensible. There was a scream in front of the cell where I fell. Probably someone had seen me fall through the edge of the door where prisoners usually stare at the corridor for hours. Anyway, three men came and threw a blanket on the ground, grabbed my hands and feet, put me on the blanket, lifted me up and took me to the medical centre of Ward 209. After taking an ECG, they gave me some injections.

From that night on, whenever these things happened, I was injected, while my condition grew worse by the day. The doctor supplied some pills for them to give me every night. The guards would give me the pills with a glass of water. Once I fainted while I was going downstairs for interrogation, and I suddenly fell down to the last step on my back. The interrogator was in front of me and, as a rule, could not prevent me from falling. I tried my best to get up on my feet or pull my legs out from under my body. I felt as if I had no bones or nerves in my legs. It was a terrible state. I was scared when I got like this. I didn't fear death, or contracting a disease. I was afraid of the unexplainable things that were happening to me in those silent, abandoned cells. Several men came again, spread the blanket, put me on it and took me up the stairs to the medical centre.

The doctor said they should give me an injection and I protested and refused. I wanted to get up but I couldn't, and I fell off the bed as I moved. I grabbed the bed leg to stand up. Suddenly the doctor took my wrist firmly in his hands and forced me on back on the tiles. My wrist hit the floor and was hurt. I started shouting. 'Bring a chain,' the doctor said, 'and tie her hands and feet to the bed legs.' He told the nurse to inject the serum. I couldn't fight against their strength and I remained motionless on the floor while they did this. They had closed the doors while I was shouting so that my voice would not get out, because the medical room was opposite the men's ward.

One day I came out of the toilet and was walking towards the cell when I suddenly fell. The same violent doctor gave a syringe to the prison guard and said, 'Inject.' But the guard said he couldn't accept the responsibility. 'Tell your nurse to inject it.' The nurse immediately did so. How could I have any confidence in the doctor, the nurse and the drugs, which only ever increased? When they all clearly distrusted each other, how could a helpless, sick prisoner have any faith in them? They both stood over my head while the nurse gave me the injection. The doctor, despite the fact that he had sworn an oath to save patients' lives, began to speak loudly. 'Ms Mohammadi. Die, but die out of the prison,' he said. 'To hell with your death, but don't make the regime pay the price for it like that woman Zahra Kazemi.'[12]

I stared at him speechlessly while lying on the ground. I doubted that he was a doctor and I still question everything that happened to me in that cell and that ward. Evin Prison

12 Zahra 'Ziba' Kazemi-Ahmadabadi, an Iranian-Canadian photographer, was arrested and brutally killed by Iranian interrogators in 2003.

Medical Centre and even my interrogators were aware of my blood tests through the letters of my doctors, Mr Hassan Gogol (my gynaecologist) and others, and knew that I'd had pulmonary embolism at the time of delivery. I had miraculously survived, and Ali and Kiana, who were less than eight months old, were born premature due to my condition. After delivery, a nuclear radiograph showed that my lungs were also damaged, and I was treated with heparin and warfarin pills for two years. My doctor had written that I should not be confined in closed, sedentary, poorly venti-lated environments, but scant attention was paid. In the cell I experienced severe shortness of breath and pain in the chest area.

Shortness of breath made me put my nose and mouth against the cranny of the door to get some oxygen. Breathing was impossible in the cell. One day I was lying asleep on the floor as I couldn't breathe properly when the guard came and helped me to go to the small yard behind the toilet, which had a glass roof. I repeatedly asked to be referred to my doctor, but this never happened. They said they had a doctor. They did have a doctor, but his behaviour did not differ from the violent interrogators. One day after my release I was hospitalized because of my grave ill health. Following the first test results, the doctors decided to inject heparin and prescribed warfarin – just as they did after my pregnancy. I used warfarin for a while. Long after my release I had trou-ble speaking. My voice would cut out against my will and I would continue after a pause. My family was intensely worried. Or when talking I would cough so much that I had to stop.

While I was in Ward 2, Sarah Shourd and two young American men who had been locked up for a long time were in the same ward. I sometimes heard her voice.[13] I heard her crying, too. Once I heard two young men call to Sarah as they were being taken down the hallway to the yard for fresh air. Sarah answered. Sarah's fiancé had stood in the doorway when the male prison guard shouted. 'Get on, don't stop, leave the door open.' He loudly told Sarah that he loved her. It saddened me when I heard Sarah's voice; I really felt sorry for her and I cried.

I searched the cell for long hours, under the carpet, on the carpet, on the walls, in the corners. What was I supposed to do? When I looked at the walls, I found some writing: a note from Shiva Nazar Ahari[14] congratulating herself on her birthday, and an article by Badralsadat Mofidi[15] who had signed her name. Badralsadat later said she had carved her name with a nail clipper.

Days passed and I had not heard a word of Ali and Kiana and not seeing them bothered me so much that sometimes I thought of dying. How much I needed to be

13 Sarah Shourd, and her partner (later fiancé) Shane Bauer, and their friend Joshua Fattal were detained by Iranian border guards while on holiday in Iraqi Kurdistan. Shourd spent over a year in solitary confinement.

14 Shiva Nazar Ahari is a human rights activist and a founding member of the Committee of Human Rights Reporters.

15 Badralsadat Mofidi is the secretary of the Iranian Journalists' Union.

and breathe in a healthy and safe environment, and how much I needed mundane things such as seeing the sun, staring at the sky, seeing a stray cat, a leaf falling from a tree, smelling good, a sound even if disruptive and unpleasant, talking to a friend, and anything that was a sign of being alive. It's impossible to imagine how not seeing the sun, not feeling the breeze on your skin and the unbroken silence around you shatters the human will to fight and keep living. An idealistic fighter can never even imagine that being deprived of the things they take for granted outside might at one point cause doubt or indifference in a passionate and productive person.

The conditions of the cell and the interrogations are mechanisms designed to overwhelm everything key to your identity and exert psychological pressure. It leaves a crack in a part of the human mind. During this time, I was in a cell with a girl named Zeynab Jalalian[16] for several days. She was a Kurdish girl. One day I saw a scar on her head and asked if something had happened to her. She said she had been in imprisoned in Kurdistan for – if I am not mistaken – six months. In that cell in Kurdistan, the interrogator once hit her on the head with a cast iron pipe leaving a deep gash in her skull. They took her to the hospital and then left her in the cell again. She told me that her cell was completely dark,

16 Zeynab Jalalian is a Kurdish Iranian originally sentenced to death by an Islamic Revolutionary Court in 2008 for being a member of the Kurdish militant PJAK, which she denies. Her sentence was commuted to life in prison in 2011.

with no window or light. Once she was brushing her teeth and preparing to sleep when the prison guard called her and took her to the yard. Zeynab said the sun was up, but she had thought it was midnight.

Two or three days of companionship with her were a boon for me. She was taken from Kurdistan to Ward 209 and they repeatedly demanded she give interviews and say that she had taken part in armed operations. She had refused to give interviews and to lie. During Zeynab's stay in Ward 209 she told interesting stories about some prisoners, which gave me a better idea of prison cells in Iran. She told of a strong woman who refused to write a letter against one of the leaders of the Green Movement despite enormous pressure, making her ill.

Seeing Zeynab and her resistant will and spirit, I saw other aspects of her character: her strength and insistence on humanist beliefs. During three periods of solitary confinement, I saw great men and women who stood with firm faith and determination despite enduring crushing pressure, and they insisted on their beliefs even at great cost to their mental and physical health.

After my release from prison on bail, I was immediately hospitalized and treated. And after my discharge, the security agents took my medical records away from the hospital. I asked the reason for this in the interrogations I had later, and the interrogator replied, 'We have doctors in the Ministry of Intelligence who are more experienced than your doctors.' This had a special meaning to me. My main interrogator was familiar with my moods, interests and the things that bothered me. He knew everything, including my habit of always chewing something and, in his own words, the way I write, my relationship with my friends at the Iranian Engineering Inspection Company, and even my relationship with my husband. Why was he so familiar with my spirit and why did he have such a thorough knowledge of it? Well, he intended to manipulate the diseases, drugs and treatments, and the weaknesses of my body, soul and mind because, as he said, they weren't done with me yet.

Third experience, May 2012

It had been two months since Taghi had left Iran, and threats from the Ministry of Intelligence forced me to leave my home in Tehran and go to Zanjan, to my parents' house, with Ali and Kiana, who were nearly five and a half. One morning, some plainclothes men came to my parents' house and took me away without an arrest warrant. Exactly half an hour before that my interrogator had called me from Tehran and told me to go to the Ministry of Intelligence's Zanjan office at the address he gave me. I had refused. That's when they came to arrest me.

First, I was taken to a building without any signboards at the entrance. We entered, and I was kept there for about four hours, until two men and a woman put me in a car and we left for Tehran. When I'd been taken from my parents' house, I'd told them to tell the truth if they were arresting me. 'No, not at all,' said the woman who was with them. 'I swear they'll just have a few questions to ask you.' Ali and Kiana behaved strangely, understanding the terrifying atmosphere. Ali raced to fetch his yellow toy rifle then grabbed hold of my coat. Kiana, who was wearing a beautiful skirt, clung to me and said, 'Mama, don't leave us alone, we will come with you.' Separating from the children was much harder than last time. I felt like my heart tore apart.

When the car drove into Evin Prison and I was handed over to Ward 209, the female agent, who had promised there would be only a few questions, was with me. 'You have children yourself,' I told her. In the car on the way to Tehran I had heard her talk to her child and promise her that she would come home in the evening. 'Did you see my children? Why did you lie to me? If you had told the truth, I couldn't have done anything about it, but at least I could have hugged and kissed them and not promised them that I would be back soon.'

My third experience started in a cell. Well, I was left alone in the cell with almost no interrogation. The next day I was taken to the women's ward and I was only there for one night, and was then returned to the cells in Ward 209. A few months before my arrest, when I was still in Tehran and Taghi had not yet left the country, the Ministry of Intelligence in Suhrawardi Street asked me to leave Iran illegally. I refused. After Taghi left, the pressure from the Ministry of

Intelligence to make me leave Iran increased. I did not want to leave. I once said I had two young children. The mountains of Kurdistan weren't safe for them and we could not go. 'Says who?' My interrogator said. 'You can go by car and it is so scenic.' I knew what I was being punished for.

On one occasion I had an interrogator who was a middle-aged man. As he put it, he had served abroad before the events of 2009. For some reason he had returned to Iran that year, and he threatened that he wouldn't let me be imprisoned in the general ward of Evin Prison. 'Rest assured,' he said, 'you'll be transferred to an ordinary prison in a small town where you can understand what it means to defend human rights and women.' I had received six years in prison and the sentence didn't mention exile to another city, so I didn't take this threat seriously. My cell's confined space had the same function as my two previous stays. Closing the iron door behind me darkened the world. Although this was my third time in prison and I was familiar with the environment in Ward 209, my reaction was the same as the first time.

I avoided thinking about Ali and Kiana. Their absence was unbearable. When their names came into my mind, I got up and ran on the spot. It felt like if I stayed still, I would break down in grief. I was sure the kids were going through hard times. I prayed to God that they would forget me. I asked that the word 'mother' not be pronounced by them. I, who had been with Ali and Kiana around the clock, had ended up in a situation that merely thinking about them, even only their names, terrified me to the point that I tried to escape from it.

The first time I blamed myself was in Ishratabad's cells. I thought my faith and convictions weren't strong enough. If they were strong, what had happened wouldn't have happened. Sometimes I thought that the problem was that I was an open, sociable and happy person. I blamed myself; if I had been a little more alone with myself in the house and practised solitude, I could have done better now in the cell and it could have been easier. My joy in exercising, pursuing my interests and having fun made it hard for me to put up with prison conditions, but I was confident in my beliefs and my ideas, my political and ideological convictions. I did not regret my actions.

Shortly after my second release I went to a psychologist who had recently published an article about solitary confinement and white torture in *Aftab* magazine. He explained to me that faith and beliefs must be separated from the body's strength and health. He told me how different individuals acted in completely different ways when it came to white torture, and perhaps these explanations could help me stop blaming myself. But the reality of my negative reaction to the cell originated in my character and could not be explained by the tools of science alone.

My body could not bear it. For a few hours during the day, the pressure on my heart was so enormous that it felt like a heavy, black object had crushed it. I had palpitations that were sometimes so strong that I could not move, sit or stand still. My breathing problems increased, and I used an inhaler several times a day, but it did not help. It had become warmer and there was no air conditioning. One night, before they gave me my medication, I was preparing to go to bed when my whole body became numb, and I could not stand on my feet. I was not in pain, but I was extremely scared and my fear was worse than enduring pain. The female prison guard came in with my medication, but when she saw me in that condition, she called three men who came with a blanket and took me to the ward's medical centre.

A doctor came and examined me. I don't remember how many injections I received. There was a nurse in the room who insisted that I get up and walk a bit. His words irritated me. He talked as if he was completely ignorant about the care that should be provided to a patient. He went on and got on my nerves. I sat on the edge of the bed to get up, but it didn't work. He insisted that I could, but I didn't want to. This so-called nurse's behaviour was inhumane. He knowingly tried to provoke me at a time when I needed some comfort and probably a sedative. There is a difference in the way doctors and nurses talk in a normal hospital and the manner of those (especially the sadistic ones) who work in prison cells. Their actions become part of the cell's identity and are so destructive.

One day a female prison guard questioned me. During the interrogation there was a lot of talk about Ali and Kiana, and I was overwhelmed by the thought of them. When I was about to leave the interrogation cell, I heard the voice of the female prison guard. 'Come here,' she said. I turned to her as if I had seen an acquaintance, and I asked her if she had

children. I still can't believe how her icy answer moved me.
'None of your business whether I do or don't,' she said. I
realized that the cell and the security ward were not just a
physical-geographical location, but that there were certain
concrete psychical, mental and human characteristics that
shape the cell and give it its meaning; prison guards' spirit-
less and rude voices, dead cockroaches on the dusty floors,
dirty and dark hanging curtains, blindfolds on the accused
eyes, bare feet in big slippers, inappropriate, poor quality
clothes, metal grilles called windows, sitting for long periods
against the wall in interrogation cells, confrontation with
people, screams and angry voices, doctors' indifference to
the condition of their patients, dry and heavy sounds of the
cell doors slamming shut, being blindfolded even inside the
ward and corridors on the way from the cell to the toilet, and
so on.

On another occasion I woke up in the morning, had a little
bread and tea for breakfast, and stood up to take a few steps
around the cell. I went maybe two or three times in circles
and then everything went dark. When I opened my eyes, I
saw women and men staring at me, female prison guards,
the security chief for the ward, nurses and doctors. One
thing I still wonder is why I was not at all surprised that so
many people were standing around me. I did not ask a single
question about what they were doing there or why I was
lying on the floor. No reaction. I did not think at all about
the fainting and coming to. I was not even afraid. I got up
and got ready and sat there again. Doctors took my pulse

and recorded my blood pressure. They talked to each other and left the cell. The night before this incident, when the female prison guard handed me my medication, I discovered a new kind of tablet and asked her what it was. She replied that the prison doctor had said that I should take it to prevent what had happened to me a few nights earlier when I went numb and couldn't stand. So, I'd taken the tablet. I cannot say for certain why I became unconscious, though, because they did not perform any blood tests on me and I was not allowed to leave the ward for further examination.

Every other day in Ward 209, we were allowed out in the fresh air for fifteen to twenty minutes. Every other day we had a shower, and we got no food other than the three meals. It had been almost a month since I had left Ali and Kiana. In the ward there were no regular routines for visits and calls. The interrogator decided these. I repeatedly wrote complaints and asked if I was sentenced to six years in prison and why they were keeping me in solitary confinement. I said that I had to be transferred to the public ward and that it was illegal for the Ministry of Intelligence to keep me in solitary confinement.

During the call to prayer one evening, an agent took me to the Shahid Moghaddas Prosecutor's Office. Mr Reshteh Ahmadi's[17] agent and secretary did not enter the room. Mr Ahmadi was sitting behind his desk. The courtroom was

17 Seyyed Bahram Reshteh Ahmadi is the deputy prosecutor for security and the head of the Evin Security Court.

empty and deserted. The head of the court listened to my complaints and agreed. He said that he'd issue an order to transfer me to a public ward and started writing. The phone rang and he answered. 'She is here with me,' he said, 'you're causing us serious problems.' And he hung up. Then he turned to me and gave me the letter to sign. I wondered why I, as the accused, should sign the order instead of the Head of the Prosecutor's Office, and he replied that it was because it was my own request. I thought that Mr Ahmadi was a responsible person in the judiciary. I was in a court of law and he was not an anonymous security agent and I wasn't being interrogated in a cell or in the security department of a prison. So, I trusted him and signed the letter. The content of the letter was about my six-year prison sentence and my transfer from Ward 209 to a women's public ward. 'Which women's ward do you mean?'

'Where there are women,' he said, pointing to somewhere outside the room.

I returned to the cell and two days later at six in the morning two male agents woke me up and we got in a car. I had to bend my head down behind the car seat and we left the prison. After many hours of driving on the highway, we arrived at the city court of Zanjan and there they handed me over to the head of the women's public ward. I was shocked and did not understand why they treated me that way. I felt like a hostage. I experienced total insecurity and no guarantee of my future. I felt dizzy from the pressure and uncertainty. I entered the quarantine ward of Zanjan

Prison, a dark, dirty and stinking room. I went to wash my hands but there was no soap or towel in the toilet, and neither was there any soap, shampoo, underwear or a towel in the shower. Not a single thing. There were only three stinking blankets in the cell, and you could see traces of vomit on them.

We got tasteless rice and vegetables for lunch, which I refused to eat. I drank water straight from the tap and there was nothing to eat. Next to my cell was a woman who had been sentenced to five years in prison for drug trafficking. She had just returned from a prison furlough and had to stay a few days in the quarantine cell. I heard a girl's voice and asked her how old she was. 'Twelve,' she replied. 'Why are you here?' I asked. She said that she had a relationship with the neighbour's boy and that her father had reported the incident to the police, and the police had brought her there. The beautiful little girl called me Aunt Narges from that day, and every time I hugged her my heart broke. At the start of my relocation to the public ward I had no room, so I slept on the floor in the prayer room. The little girl was with me and at night she grabbed my hands hard because she was scared, and I kissed her head and cheeks and talked to her all the time.

In the city of Zanjan, I came to understand that the reason for my transfer to the public ward of Zanjan Prison had been the letter I had signed in Mr Reshteh Ahmadi's office. I had seen the letter. It turned out that Mr Ahmadi had forged and added a sentence to the letter after my signature when I had left the room; 'Ali and Kiana are in Zanjan.' Colluding with the Ministry of Intelligence, they had pretended my relocation to Zanjan was my own request. What happened to me in Zanjan Prison is suffused with unlimited and indescribable suffering and pain. As a result, I have permanent convulsions. The Ministry of Intelligence later classified this information in all my medical records during my stay in Valieasr Hospital. Sometimes blisters of wounds from the solitary confinement burst, sometimes they fester, sometimes they burn and sometimes fear leaks into my veins. There is still no end to the invisible and unhealed wounds.

NIGARA AFSHARZADEH

Nigara Afsharzadeh (born 1978) is a citizen of Turkmenistan. She was arrested in 2014 in Mashhad on charges of espionage and sentenced to five years in prison. Nigara spent a year and a half in solitary confinement in Ward 209, Evin Prison, and was later transferred to the women's ward.

When and how were you arrested?

I was arrested on 6 January 2014 in Mashhad by two men and two women. I was on the street with my two children, aged six and eight. I had come to Iran to see my daughter. I had separated from her father, then one day he phoned me and told me to come to Iran and take my daughter with me to Turkmenistan. When I arrived, I realized that this was a trap. I was arrested on the street with my two young children. When they separated me from them, I was not told what would happen to them. Interrogators said the children had been taken to an orphanage.

Where were you taken when you were arrested?

I was transferred to a cell. The cell was dark, and I had only one blanket. I stayed in that cell for a day and a night. The next day they came to me. They wanted to put a sack on my head, which I resisted. I did not let them. When we got in the car, they pushed my head down to my feet so that I could not see anything. They didn't feed me while I was in the cell, they gave me food when I got on the plane, but I couldn't eat anything.

Where did they take you when you arrived in Tehran?

They blindfolded me so I didn't know where I was going. When I opened my eyes, I was in a cell. Above my head were two lights. There were three blankets and a thin carpet on the floor of the wide cell. The cell was in corridor three, Ward 209 of Evin Prison, run by the Ministry of Intelligence. While I was confined in this cell, no one was in this corridor. No one passed by, there were no voices, not even the sound of a cell door opening or closing. The only living creatures in that corridor were terrifying, big cockroaches.

What did you do in the cell?

Time does not pass in the cell. I was all alone. The cell door had a narrow hatch that the women officers sometimes opened to look inside. I put my face behind the hatch for hours so that if they opened the door I could look into the corridor. The cell was silent and there was no sound. I looked all over the cell so that I might find something like an ant, and whenever I could find one, I followed it. I talked to the ant for hours. I cried, moaned and prayed for many hours. I thought that I saw some of the prophets in my dreams. I saw strange things when I slept. I could not believe them when I woke up. I walked all day every day. I walked so much that my legs were paralysed. When they brought me lunch, I would chop up the lumps of rice and throw them on the ground to attract an ant or something else, to entertain myself. I wanted a living thing in the cell with me. I was overjoyed when a fly appeared. I was careful not to let it leave when the door was open. I followed it around in the cell and talked to it.

How often did they let you out for fresh air?
How about going to the toilet and bathroom?

I had to put on the blindfold if there was any reason I needed to leave the cell. Blindfolded, I was permitted to go to the toilet a few times during the day. They yelled at me when I tried to peek out the sides of the blindfold, even when I was looking at the wall. Once a week I could have a shower.

The women officers who were standing behind the door would get angry, shout and tell me to get out. I said my body stank. 'Let it stink,' they said, 'cooperate with the interrogators to make things better.'

I could go to the prison yard twice a week for twenty minutes. The wall was too high to see over and the yard had no flowers or plants.

What about your health, and did you receive medical treatment?

I ate almost nothing. The officers would say that I was going to be their guest for a long time, but I had no appetite to eat. Soon I lost weight. When I was arrested, I was 70 kg and after a few months I was down to 53 kg.

After a while, a black liquid came out of my nipples, and I still suffer from this condition. From the very first days, I suffered from insomnia and anxiety. I felt awful. They took me to a room and said that this was the health centre of Ward 209. Someone examined me and prescribed some medicine. From the first days they gave me eight pills and told me to take them to get well, but I really did not sleep at night. I would stay awake for hours. The morning call to prayer would come and I would still be awake. I could not sleep at all.

I was always awake, and frustrated because I was alone and had nothing to do. Sometimes I did not notice the passage of time. There was a button in the cell that I pushed when I wanted to go to the toilet. Over and over again I pushed that button, and when they opened the door, I saw that they were sleepy. I asked them how they cooked a certain kind of broth or some other food. You cannot imagine how angry they got. They shouted and slammed the door. 'It is now three or four o'clock in the morning,' they would say, 'why don't you sleep and let us sleep?' But I wondered why they were asleep. I didn't know when it was time to sleep. I pressed the button for no reason except to see a living creature. I was in that cell for a year and a half. I slept on the rough military blankets. I didn't have a pillow and all this time I had a military blanket under my head and pulled another over my body. Purulent wounds developed on my sides and back, but the more I complained about it, the less they listened. They gave me a blouse and pants, and every time I went to the bathroom, they gave me another set of the same to change into. The blankets were so rough that my bones ached when I slept on my side, but I had no choice.

How were the interrogations?

The first day that they took me to the interrogation cell in Tehran there were two interrogators: one young and one relatively middle-aged. They said that this was the end. 'Think that this is the grave?' They said, 'You are dead, and we are Munkar and Nakir.'[1] I did not even understand what

---

1 Munkar and Nakir are two angels that question the deceased on their faith in Islam.

they were saying. I used to say to myself, 'Well, which one is Munkar, and which one is Nakir?' They asked questions I did not know the answers to. They told me to go and to call them whenever I remembered what I had done. I was not in a good mental state, because I was very worried about my children. I was told that they had been left in the middle of the street and had to be taken to an orphanage. Distressed, I did not know what to do. I didn't touch the food. They would get angry and say, 'Are you on strike?' 'What is a strike?' I asked.

I got different diseases there, and was so sick that they gave me psychiatric medication. One day the interrogator came in and said, 'You are accused of espionage. You should confess to the things you have done in Iran.'

I was blindfolded during the interrogations and could only hear their voices. When they pretended to be angry, they hurled things at me, tea boxes and other things. Once, one of them kicked my chair hard from behind. 'You are a liar,' he said.

Sometimes there were just the same two interrogators, but sometimes there were more. Once I guessed from their voices that up to five people were behind me. They gave me a glass of water once. 'Pour it on the ground,' one of them ordered. I did so. 'Now gather it with your hands.' I tried. 'Spilled water cannot be collected again,' he said.

I did not understand what they said. Once an interrogator blew his nose on a paper towel and threw it on the ground. He said that women are like this paper towel, they are to be used and then thrown away. Sometimes interrogation took a long time, lasting from morning to night. They ate lunch and dinner there. They gave me the same food, but I could not eat anything. The interrogator threatened me all the time. 'You'll be in the cell until your hair is as white as your teeth,' he said. 'We will have you skinned. You will be hanged and I myself will pull the stool from under your feet.' Once he said, 'Your grandmother came to Iran to look after you and we arrested her because she is also a spy.' Another time they said, 'Your grandmother is dead.'

I love my grandmother indescribably. When they told me she was dead, I went to the cell and wept so hard. I performed the third, seventh and fortieth ceremonies[2] for her. One day the interrogator said, 'Eldar [my six-year-old son] is terribly ill and has been taken to the hospital. He needs a kidney. He is dying.'

I was so overwhelmed with grief that I could not bear it. My mobile phone, which had photos of my children on it, was in the hands of the interrogators. They printed Eldar's photo, but there was something white hanging on his chest, like a card, and something like a rope around his neck. I felt sick when they gave it to me. I was asked to write on the white part. They made me write the word 'wretched' on my son's chest. From then, whenever they interrogated me, they put photos of both my children in front of me so that I saw them

2 Ceremonies held for the dead on the third, seventh and fortieth day of their death, in Iran.

all the while. One day they came and said they were going to Mashhad. I asked why. 'Your mother has come after your children and we are going to detain her and bring her here,' they said. Believe me, I thought my mother had actually been brought to the ward. I could even hear her voice.

They questioned me about things I had no idea about. I didn't know what to write. They put a piece of paper in front of me and told me to write the names of the boys I had talked to since my childhood. Once, one of the interrogators got angry and pulled out his gun and started threatening me. They swore at me and insulted me during the interrogations.

They forced me to describe my sexual relations with Mr Kh. They asked me, not once or twice, but over and over again to explain our intercourse in detail. This part of the interrogation was especially offensive. Several times the interrogators took me to a hotel and filmed me. They would bring me a headscarf and overcoat to wear. They wanted me to say, without saying what country I am from, that we women 'in other countries' try to seduce the officials of the Islamic Republic of Iran into sexual relations. They told me to warn Iran's agents that women like me seduce them and the moment they're enticed, we start to spy on them. I had this 'interview' several times.

I had my mobile phone with me when I was arrested, and now it was in the hands of the interrogators. They looked at all my photos, even the private ones, and asked questions about them. Even a judge in the court had them, and I

objected that these photos were completely private, for example photos of my husband, my children and me. I asked why
they had access to them.

Were you able to contact your family?

For six months I did not hear from anyone, not from my
mother or from my two young children. I was going crazy.
The interrogator said that this was like a grave. I started
to believe it. Anyway, after six months they gave me a
phone and I called my eldest daughter, who was in Iran.
They said she could come and visit me, and she did. I asked
about my little ones. She said that my mother had come
from Turkmenistan and taken them. After eight months,
they allowed me to call my mother on the phone. I had
believed my grandmother was dead. I had believed that
my children had been taken to an orphanage and my
husband had left me. Then I realized that these were all
lies.

How often did they interrogate you and for how long?

In the early days, two or three times a week. After a while
the interrogators came once a week. And then they came
after long intervals. I was left in the cell. I was not a spy. The
interrogator said that they knew that I did not spy, but that I
had to cooperate with them and say what they told me to say
in the interview. They said that if I cooperated, they would

give me money to bring my little children to Iran and live here. They said they would harass me if I returned to my home country. 'Stay here,' they said. And I wondered why they wouldn't continue to punish me since they had arrested and detained me on espionage charges already. Why would they give me money, a house and a residence permit?

How would you describe the changes in your mental and physical conditions during that year and a half?

I could not eat food. Over time I became emaciated. Lying on the floor caused severe back pain, and because I was confined to that cramped cell and deprived of mobility, my digestive system worked poorly. I was constipated and it hurt. They gave me only one or two pieces of fruit a week.

I was in the cell throughout the winter. There was a thin rug on the floor and I put a military blanket under me. I felt like I was freezing. My body froze and it wouldn't warm up, no matter what I did. I drank the tap water. Later I realized that Evin Prison's water was not safe to drink. I had now become physically weak, and I felt terrible mentally. I cried so much that I suffered from severe pain in my eyes. I had an awfully bad toothache, but nothing was done for me in terms of treatment. About eight months later, when I was taken to the hospital, there was a mirror inside the elevator where I saw my face. I was very saddened and shocked to see my reflection.

What did you do to pass the time in the cell?

A year and a half of solitary confinement was devastating. I felt dizzy when I heard the bell ring in the hallway. I was sick and tired of hearing the rest of the prisoners leave while I had to stay in my cell. It embittered me to hear the voices of men and women crying loudly in the hallway. Once I heard a young boy who was being beaten. He begged them not to beat him. He said he was sick. I cried so much that my head ached. I was so overwhelmed by loneliness that I started doing strange things. For example, I would put the bread they gave me to eat in my mouth and chew it until it was soft. Then I made a doll and a cross for my little son, but as soon as I went to the bathroom, they came in the cell and destroyed them.

What bothered you the most?

It was horrible for me to imagine my children in an orphanage. I was really going insane. They were small and I'd been forced to leave them out on the street. My daughter cried and told me not to go. I have not yet seen them. During interrogations, insults and derogatory comments made me incredibly angry. Some of my interrogations were about my sexual relationships. I could not believe they asked a woman such questions. The interrogator once wanted me to talk about a man to whom I had been temporarily married.[3] 'Describe

3 Nigara uses the word *sigheh*, a private marriage contract licit in Twelver Shia Islam, in which the length of the marriage and dowry is determined in advance.

your sexual intercourse,' he said. No matter what I said, he would keep insisting. I asked him what he did with his wife when they had sex. 'We did the same things,' I said. 'No,' he said, 'you should show me how you did it and describe it.' So, I did it. He then asked if we used honey. I think they had secretly recorded our phone calls because the man they referred to was Iranian and we'd sometimes spoken on the phone. The interrogator knew about some of the things we had talked about. He asked about the honey repeatedly until I answered, 'Yes, we used honey.' Then he told his colleagues to send a certain man and the woman to the cell and give them honey. I did not know what to do in such instances except go back to the cell and pray. Once I prayed eighty rak'ats at a time and fainted. I called all the prophets and asked them to help me. The worst things were the silence and solitude – they drove me insane. It was a dreadful time.

ATENA DAEMI

Atena Daemi, a civil rights activist, was arrested on 30 October 2014 by the Intelligence division of Sarollah Camp of IRGC,[1] and transferred to Ward 2A of the IRGC Detention Centre in Evin Prison.

The children's rights activist was charged with 'insulting the supreme leader', 'insulting the sacred', 'conspiracy to disrupt national security', and 'concealing evidence of a crime'. She was detained in Ward 2A for eighty-six days and then transferred to the women's general ward. Atena was sentenced to five years in prison on charges of conspiracy and two years in prison on charges of insulting the leadership.

1 The Islamic Revolutionary Guard Corps (IRGC) is one branch of the Iranian Armed forces.

What was the condition of your cell?

I was arrested, and then after six hours of inquisition I entered Evin Prison, which I had never thought about before. I was taken past a few doors and then put in a cell. It was about three metres by two metres. There was a window that was high up and had several layers of grilles which completely prevented light from entering the cell, but the blue colour of the sky could still be seen through its holes. Inside the cell, there was a yellow light bulb and a white one, both on the ceiling. When it was time to sleep, they turned off the white light. The walls of the cell were covered with marble up to the height of a human, and the rest was cream-coloured plaster. The cell door was iron and pea-coloured. At the bottom of the door there was a hatch. I'd put a strip of paper out to say that I needed to go to the bathroom. The floor of the cell was covered with a thin, machine-made carpet. I had two blankets for sleeping and one blanket to use as a pillow. I was in this cell for about thirty days.

What was the difference between this cell and the next one?

After thirty days I was transferred to a larger cell, which was twice the size of the previous one. From the traces left on the wall, one could guess that two cells had been joined. There was no toilet in the previous cell, but in the new cell there was a toilet that was separated from the rest of the cell by a door. There was a little sugar and salt inside the cell and there were three lights. The window was right up by the ceiling, but instead of opening to outside the building it opened into the corridor, where there was no light or sound. The corridor was pitch black. It was the way to enter and exit Section 2A and the interrogation rooms.

How was your mental and psychological state?

I was arrested in the alley. After searching my father's house and then my sister's house, they took me to my workplace, and then to my cell. The sound of the door being slammed shut behind me devastated me. I knew I had been deprived of the right to control my own life.

It was crushing. There was absolute silence. I turned and looked at the closed door. I felt trapped inside a matchbox. I thought that this door would not open, except by the request of the interrogator. After each interrogation I said to myself, 'Maybe I will be interrogated tomorrow and maybe not.' I felt conflicted. You didn't know which one you'd prefer; that they opened the door and interrogated you, or that they locked it forever without interrogating you. The first night, when one of the lights went out, I subconsciously jumped up and called out to them, asking what they were doing. 'Silence,' they said. 'Sleep now!'

I heard the morning call to prayer at dawn; I had not slept. I could not sleep. The place was unfamiliar and sickening to me. It was the first time in my life that I was not at home with my parents. I didn't know what had happened to them and what they were doing. I didn't know what would happen tomorrow. I wanted to smoke but they wouldn't give me a cigarette. There was nothing to entertain you, not even for a minute. I was always waiting for something to happen. I was oblivious to everything and everyone. Everything was vague and undecided. The wait was deadly. In solitary confinement it's only your mind that works. Sometimes I thought about the issues raised during the interrogation. Sometimes I thought about my reactions to the interrogators' behaviour, and I planned accordingly, but eventually there came a time when these thoughts became exhausting. I didn't know what to do.

I liked to sleep and not think about anything, because the truth was bitter enough. Thinking about things and going over them made me even more bitter. That is why I struggled between sleeping and staying awake. I didn't trust anything, and I didn't know what would happen.

What changed the mood, even for a few minutes?

Frequently, I tried to think of things I had taken for granted before my arrest. It was very curious that I missed all of them. I tried to dissect the past. I tried to remember the books I had read or my favourite songs. The first few days I thought no one could hear me. One day the sound of banging on the wall caught my attention. It was an eerie sound, but at least it was a sound that had broken the silence. I realized that there was someone on the other side of the wall. I jumped up and tried to communicate with those around me in other cells. I did the same thing when I was taken outside for open air hour. Either way, I made my presence known. This encouraged other prisoners to do the same. All of this was fun and entertaining for a few minutes only. There was nothing in the cell to change the atmosphere.

Everything was uniform and monotonous. In the cell, especially at night, I heard loud noises. I didn't know why men shouted. I felt like they were torturing someone. It was a bad feeling. Fear, worry and sadness consumed my whole being and the cell space became more unfamiliar and unfathomable. I later found out that it was the voices of the soldiers of Evin Prison who were calling each other from the watchtowers. As I laid my head on the floor, I heard a man crying from downstairs. I grew disconsolate. I tried to show him that he was not alone by knocking on the wall. He would notice and then not only did the sound of crying stop, but he also knocked in response.

The sound of the call to prayer in that ward was different from any others I had ever heard. This call to prayer and the way it was made was like the trumpet of death. It made me feel bad. I was in the cell during Muharram. The sound of *noha*,[2] crying and mourning, was played loudly every day in the ward, which strangely disturbed me.

---

2 *Noha* is a lament about the martyrdom of Hussain ibn Ali in Shia tradition.

How was the food?

They gave me bread, cheese and tea for breakfast. Sometimes they would give me milk or a piece of fruit at eleven o'clock. We had lunch at noon. In Ward 2A prisoners' fresh-air hour was once in the morning and once in the evening. Most days, as it was cold, they took me out only in the afternoon. Afterwards they would give me tea and then dinner at about six o'clock, which was usually something to eat with bread. Bedtime was eleven o'clock at night. I had no appetite but I just had to eat.

Were you arraigned immediately after the arrest?

The day I was arrested and transferred to the prison, I was taken for interrogation after changing and giving my clothes to the prison guards. I had not even seen my cell, which was two floors below. I entered a very small room that only had room for one chair. In front of the chair there was a one-way mirror.

When the door was closed, no sound came in or went out. Then the interrogation started. They brought my friend 'S' and kept her next to them. I heard and recognized the voice. They wanted to show me that my friends had also been arrested. Early the next morning they took me to the courthouse and kept me in the prayer room. I even ate lunch there. I was there until evening. The courthouse was closed, and I was taken into the corridor. We waited there until ten o'clock, when they took me to the office of an interrogator named Khorshidi. The interrogator of my case and another person who spoke in a strong

Gilaki accent were there. My interrogator read the charges and handed me the form. I think eighteen to twenty charges were listed: acting against national security, association and collusion, blasphemy, etc. I was constantly threatened with execution while reading the form.

I wrote that I did not accept any of the charges. My body, my voice and my hands were shaking. I felt so much hatred and I was trying my best to control myself. It was as if they wanted to cut me to pieces with their teeth. I knew I was alone. They lied and threatened, and I knew there was no one to help me. My sisters had also been arrested. Not knowing anything of my family and friends worried me even more. 'Do not deny anything,' they said. 'We know everything. If you cooperate, you might not be executed.' And so, they went on threatening me. When they realized that they had gone too far, one of them brought me a glass of water. At twelve o'clock I was put in a car. The Gilak man made it seem as if he knew all my relatives. He talked in Gilaki[3] to me. I did not answer. I only later found out that he was from Gilan.

How did you spend your time in the cell?

When I woke up in the morning, I tried to drink tea slowly to pass the time. I would pick up any crumbs and put them into the tea. I would collect whatever strands of my curly hair had fallen on to the floor. The comb they gave me could hardly go

3 Spoken in Iran's Gilan Province. Atena originally comes from Gilan.

through my hair and it took me a long time to untangle the knots. I spent part of my time doing this. I would roll up the blankets and lean on them and look at the stones on the wall. I tried to find shapes in the marble of the walls. I was bored.

I threw dry bread to the ants. After lunch I slept a little and then carved shapes on the lunch dish with a spoon. It was cold, and my legs ached or went numb. I felt severe dizziness and it got worse as I walked around the room. It was as if the walls were attacking me.

There was a cutting from a newspaper that a former prisoner had pasted on the wall with toothpaste, and I don't know how many hundreds of times I read it. I had memorized the writings, names and poems other prisoners had written on the wall. When I got a pen after fifty days, I filled all the walls with the poems I liked.

How was your health?

Every other day, there was an opportunity to have a bath. There was a hall with a camera at the top, and in front of it were four bathrooms with only two for prisoners. There was a hanger next to the door. When I was in the bathroom, I was constantly worried that the video camera would record me.

The bath time was twenty minutes, but I needed half an hour just to wash my hair, especially since there was no proper shampoo and conditioner and we bathed with liquid soap. They were extremely strict. To go to the toilet and the bathroom, for as long as I was in the cell without a toilet, I had to put a piece of paper out of the hatch so that they could open the door when they saw it. They often took hours to come and then they said I had no right to knock on the door! I did not drink water at night because they said they would not open the door then.

What was the atmosphere like during the interrogations?

I saw both interrogators at my home during the arrest. One of them, who wrote the questions, was the more flexible, so to speak, and the other was the more severe. The weather was cold, and the interrogation rooms were cold. From the beginning of my detention, I said that I had the right to remain silent and that I would use it. They threatened and insulted me with obscenities. All of a sudden, they'd make strange noises to frighten me. Once they said something inappropriate. I stood up and told them to take me back to my cell. They said they would not come to interrogate me and that my case would remain unresolved. 'Good,' I said. I went to the cell and they did not come for two days. After several days of futile attempts to make me confess, another person came into the room. They called him Sardar.[4] He spoke respectfully.

4 Sardar is the honorific title used for officers ranked Second Brigadier General and higher in the Islamic Revolutionary Guard Corps, and police commanders who have previously served in the former military or the Islamic Revolution Committees, as well as the commanders of the disbanded Jihad of Construction.

I told him that I had the right to remain silent and that I would not come to the interrogation if the interrogators insulted me, not even to say that I had the right to remain silent. He said the interrogators made a mistake and then he turned to them and told them 'Let her be silent, we have enough evidence against her.' Then he left.

On the seventeenth or eighteenth day of interrogation I was taken to another, larger room. There were many chairs facing the wall, a window on the left and a table on the right. I was alone in the room. Then I saw that one of my friends had been brought in and she was questioned. She answered and left. Then they brought another friend of mine and asked her questions, and she left. The interrogators realized that they had put me under a lot of pressure. The same day I was given a cigarette and a phone for the first time. I was shocked. They had traumatized me the worst way possible, but I tried to respond to their actions with contempt and ridicule, citing their own rules. It invigorated me and made them even angrier. They tried to create divisions between my friends and I. I was confronted with my friends several times, but I didn't accept what the interrogators claimed about them. They hadn't yet been able to access my laptop, email and password-protected accounts, and due to my denials and silence, I was charged with concealing evidence.

How many days did the interrogations take?

I had about forty-five days of interrogation. I even had interrogations on Tasua and Ashura.[5] They often gave me lunch and even dinner in the interrogation room. Some days I was not allowed to have the usual open air break due to the lengthy questioning.

After the interrogations finished, I was first given a pen and then a newspaper and a television. Twenty days after the last interrogation I was locked in a cell with Mahdieh Golroo.[6]

Before I was granted these rights, that is for fifty days, my conditions were intolerable. Even the sound of other cells' TVs bothered me, but after that the situation got a little better. At least I was not alone with the walls any more.

Were you allowed phone calls? What were the conditions for visits?

I was allowed a phone call for the first time after eighteen days and then once a week I had the right to have a phone call for four minutes. My first visit was after twenty-five days. After that, on Thursdays I had an hour-long face-to-face meeting with only three family members. The meeting took place in a small room and the interrogator would stand behind the door.

5 Tasua is the ninth day and Ashura is the tenth day of Muharram, the first month in the Islamic calendar. In Shia tradition, Ashura commemorates the martyrdom of the Prophet's grandson, Hussain ibn Ali, at the Battle of Karbala.
6 Mahdieh Golroo is a student activist and women's rights activist. She was arrested and transferred to Evin Prison a few days after a gathering of women's movement activists, in front of the Islamic Parliament on 21 October 2014, protesting the acid attacks against women in Isfahan.

How helpful was meeting with your family?

It was especially important. When I couldn't see my family, I was bothered by not knowing what was happening and this made me anxious. Meeting them allayed my worries and I would be informed about the process of the case. Meetings have an uplifting effect on the prisoner's morale. We didn't have a mirror in Ward 2A, and so it was my mother who told me how I looked.

After the interrogations, and thanks to my family's efforts, I was seen by the forensic physician of Evin Prison for my dizziness and paraesthesia. I was sent to Baqiyatallah Hospital for an MRI, but I was returned to Evin's public ward before being told the results. Due to the inhospitable conditions, including a lack of natural light and open air, alongside coercion and distress, I started to suffer from many mental and physical illnesses. I later found out that most of my fellow prisoners in these cells had the same problems.

What do you think about solitary confinement?

The solitary cell is like a sealed tin. You have no will to open the lid, and the pressure, isolation and expectations are like hammers pounding on this tin to crush it. Without warning, they suddenly open the door, slamming the lock. Anyone other than you, lying in the heart of that cell, can do this whenever they want. In all my time there, I subconsciously avoided looking at the door.

ZAHRA ZAHTABCHI

Zahra Zahtabchi (born 1969) is a sociologist and researcher in social sciences.

The Ministry of Intelligence arrested Zahra on the street on 16 October 2013. From that day until August 2014 she was kept in solitary confinement under constant interrogation. Her husband, Seyed Javad Khoshniyat Nikou, her daughter, Narges, and her sister, Faezeh, were also detained for several days at the time of her arrest, and Zahra Zahtabchi has been in prison without any leave ever since.

Her trial was held a year after arrest, on 1 August 2015. Zahra had previously been detained for several days in 2009 following a poll conducted by the University of Tehran about the results of the presidential election. In 2015 she was accused of having links to the Mujahedin-e-Khalq Organization[1] because she possessed a photo of her father,

---

1 People's Mujahedin of Iran, or the Mujahedin-e-Khalq, is an Iranian militant organization. Its primary aim is to replace the current regime with a new government.

Ali Asghar Zahtabchi, who was executed in 1981 for support-ing it. Judge Salavati sentenced Zahra to ten years in prison.

When and how were you arrested?

I was arrested on 16 October 2013 on the street. I was imme-diately sent to solitary confinement. I was handed over to Ward 209 of the Ministry of Intelligence in Evin Prison. I did not have any contact for the first thirty-three days. When I was arrested, I found out that my husband had also been arrested. Neither then, nor now, has he been politically active.

After I was handed over to the head of the operations team, I had to go with them as they searched my house. No one was home. They confiscated all my personal belongings, and then they took me to my mother's house. It was Eid, and my daughters were there. The officers arrested my sister and my eldest daughter. When we finally arrived at Evin, it was nine in the evening.

It was there that I learned my husband, sister and daugh-ter were being held in Ward 209. As soon as I reached 209, after changing my clothes, I was taken to the interrogation cell.

Javad, my sister and my daughter were being interrogated in nearby cells, and I could hear their voices. I was not allowed to contact anyone for thirty-three days.

How long were you interrogated?

During my fourteen months in solitary confinement, I had three months of interrogation. The interrogator came about once every ten days. The interrogation started at nine or ten o'clock in the morning. At lunch time I would sit in the interrogation cell so that they could go, eat lunch and come back. Interrogation usually lasted until three or four o'clock in the afternoon. I didn't have much to say during the interrogations.

When were you allowed to have phone calls?

After three months the interrogations ended, and I was allowed to call home on Sundays. When I first called, my mother said that my husband had been released after twenty days, my sister after ten days and my daughter after one day. I'd been unaware of what had happened to them. The prison arranged meetings with my family every fifteen days. I later heard that my husband had been beaten, even though he did not participate in political activities at all, nor did he have any interest in politics.

What did you do after the interrogations in prison?

Three months later, after the interrogations were over, I was granted the right to a newspaper and a television which I could use from nine a.m. to ten p.m.

Tell us about the condition of the cell.

For the first three months I was in a cell that was at the top of the building. It had an iron window that was covered from behind with a perforated metal plate that prevented light from passing through. I was in the third corridor. Those in Ward 209 knew that I was in that corridor. And they knew that the higher the corridor number, the darker and more suffocating it is, and I was in the last room. It was winter and the weather was very cold. I wrapped the blanket around myself because of the glacial chill so that I could warm up a bit. I prayed that the cell would heat up a little. I prayed that the sun would shine on the roof of the cell so that heat might come through. It was so cold that I could not get up and walk in the cell for a while. I was in the third corridor until Eid, but then Corridor Three was given to the men and they took me to Corridor One. I was the only person in that corridor. The hardships of the first three months were terrible. The food was not good for me. Even when I wanted cold water to drink, they would not give it to me and said in a disdainful tone, 'Go and drink from the tap.' They didn't even give me a broom to clean the cell. I was taken out for fresh air for twenty minutes a day on three days of the week. I could take a bath three days a week, and on Fridays I could have neither fresh air time nor a bath. I had nothing.

Tell me about the security procedures.

I did not have a toilet in the room, and I had to wear a blindfold every time I left the cell to go to the toilet. This was even though the bathroom was a few steps away. Imagine, I was in that cell for fourteen months and during these fourteen months, I had to wear a blindfold every time I wanted to go to the bathroom. For a long time, I was physically inspected every time I wanted to go to the bathroom, that is both when I went to the bathroom and when I returned to the cell. 'There is no one in this cell or the toilet except me,' I said. 'I have nothing with me neither here nor there, so why do you inspect my body?'

They did it anyway and wouldn't listen to me, no matter how much I objected. Once the head of Ward 209 came and asked if the food was good. This was the second time he asked this question. 'Sir,' I replied. 'Am I a sheep that I am always asked about the food? Consider my conditions. I have been living alone in a cell for months, and every single time I step out of the cell to go to the bathroom I undergo physical inspection. What kind of harassment is this?' I knew, however, that he was just following orders.

How was your physical condition and medical treatment?

I broke my tooth once, so I wanted to be taken to the prison's health centre. They wouldn't pay me any attention, though. My teeth had become infected, and despite my bad condition, they wouldn't take me to the health centre. One of the women guards gave me a few pills without taking me to the hospital and without a doctor's prescription, saying they were antibiotics. I had no choice. I took the pills for a few days. Some time passed and the boss of 209 came to check on my condition. I said my tooth is broken and infected, I have trouble eating and I have a toothache. 'I'll order the necessary medical treatment,' he said. One day they came and took me to the basement of the ward. I went into a room with a ping pong table and a chair. I sat on the chair. An old man came and saw my tooth and said nothing could be done and I had to put up with it. He gave me a pack of dental floss and left. My broken tooth remained untreated until the end of my solitary confinement.

How did you spend your time in the cell?

Once I asked the head interrogator to at least give me a pen and a notebook. I only had the Qur'an and the *Mafatih al-Jinan*,[2] I did not even have a copy of *Nahj al-Balagha*.[3] After a few months I applied for one and received it. I had made a schedule for myself covering the fourteen months of my solitary confinement. I read the Qur'an fourteen times during these fourteen months. Every day I read a part of the Qur'an with its translation. When I received *Nahj al-Balagha*, I

2 *Mafatih al-Jinan* (Keys to Heavens) by Abbas Qumi is a Twelver Shi'a compilation of acts of worship after prayer.
3 *Nahj al-Balagha* (The Way of Eloquence) is the most famous collection of writings attributed to Ali, cousin and son-in-law of Muhammad.

included it in my daily routine. In the mornings, after I got up for prayers, I didn't sleep, but exercised. I exercised twice a day: once in the morning and once in the evening. After morning exercise, I ate breakfast with a cup of tea served in a disposable plastic cup. Breakfast was usually a piece of bread, with a bit of jam and butter. They also gave me an egg on Fridays. Some days, like Saturday, the food was very bad and I did not eat it. I fasted every Monday and Thursday.

Every day I would draw a line on the wall to mark the days of imprisonment. I tried not to sleep too much. I read the writings of recent prisoners on the cell wall. To stop us reading them, the guards painted over the walls every few months. I memorized verses from the Qur'an during the day. I memorized three chapters of the Qur'an. Sometimes I would write things on the wall. But then one day I went to the bathroom and when I returned, the prison guard said that they'd cleaned the walls for me.

What was the justification for keeping you in solitary confinement for so long?

I was arrested on 16 October 2013. I was interrogated for three months and then left alone in my cell. My first trial was on 8 April 2014, and my last was on 7 December of the same year. The judge in the case was Salavati.[4]

---

4   Abolqasem Salavati is the head of the 15th branch of the Islamic Revolutionary Court in Tehran, and has been sanctioned by the US.

Court hearings were postponed for no reason. The first time I went to court I waited for hours for the judge to come. They said he had gone to visit his relatives and friends for Eid. I was asked if I had a lawyer. 'I do not,' I said. I was arrested on the street, and I am still kept in a cell and I don't have access to anyone.

I was entitled to a public defender. After a few months in the cell for no reason, we went to Branch 15 again. The trial was not held *again*. My interrogator, Mr Alawi, said that my case was serious and that I was charged with *moharebeh*.[5] He said that the public defender had read the case and had been so scared that he had refused to take it and had left.

My mother went from one branch of the court to another, from one prosecutor to another, pressuring them to hold the trial by asking about it. I was transferred to the Evin Women's General Ward in December 2014, and was sentenced to twelve years in prison on 11 January 2014. In the Court of Appeals, my sentence was upheld and ten years of it had to be served.

---

5 *Moharebeh* is the crime of 'waging war against God', 'war against God and the state' and 'enmity against God'. It is a capital crime in the Islamic Republic of Iran.

You were held in solitary confinement for fourteen months. Did you think you could handle such torture?

I was not politically active when I had been free, leaving aside a period of six months before my arrest, when I participated in a small activity. At this time, I was employed and worked on a project about the 2009 elections and subsequent events. It was a poll carried out for the office of the Supreme Leader. We gave people questionnaires to fill out in public places like subways and streets. It was a field study, and we asked people if they believed what was being alleged about people being tortured and killed.

One day I was working in Haft Tir subway when I noticed a gentleman standing next to me. It seemed a bit suspicious. Because I worked legally, I was sure there was no danger. I asked him to fill out the questionnaire, too. He went and I noticed that he was going to the police kiosk located in Haft Tir Square. A police officer came and arrested me. We went to the detention centre on Vozara Street. I explained that my job was administrative, and I did this according to my administrative duty. Our boss had told all of us investigators to call him right away if we had a problem, but they wouldn't let me.

I spent one night in the detention centre on Vozara Street. The night in Vozara was very tough. It was deserted in the morning but very crowded from evening onwards. Female drug addicts were brought in, and I was in another room with a woman arrested for having a temporary marriage, and a woman working in a pyramid scheme. The toilets were very dirty and terrible. They brought us food in an aluminium pot and the women thronged towards it. An awful image of prison took shape in my mind there.

Over this truly short time in prison in 2009, I accepted the reality of imprisonment and its hardships. That one night in Vozara Detention Centre was my first and only previous experience of being in prison. When I entered Ward 209 in 2013, I had a very difficult night and a very bad interrogation. I was brought to the corridor from the women's ward, and I was waiting for the interrogator when he suddenly took my chador and pulled it tight and threw me into the cell. He started threatening and insulting me. He said they would bring ten members of my family there in a few days. He insulted my family, my mother-in-law, etc. Threats and insults pervaded the atmosphere. He said, 'I received your death sentence some time ago.' I was not even allowed to speak. When I wanted to say a word, he shouted that I had no right to. The whole night passed with this atmosphere. He said, 'Bring a shroud.' Suddenly he threw a bag in front of me. I saw a few banners in it when I opened it. They also brought a photo of my father, who was executed in June 1981 that I had framed. He asked if I had connections to the Ashraf Camp.[6] 'No,' I said, 'my father and sister were killed.' They brought my laptop, printer and computer from my house.

6 Camp Ashraf was the headquarters of the Iranian opposition group Mujahedin-e-Khalq. It shut down in 2016, after its last members were flown to Albania.

I remember the first day of detention; together with the interrogators we were standing in front of Evin, waiting for an officer who was supposed to follow me home for investigation. I heard the interrogators, who knew I could hear them, saying that a certain interrogator would beat the accused before the interrogation. At which point one of the interrogators came forward and gave me the phone. It was Mr Alawi, the head interrogator. Alawi is the interrogator of the members of the organization. His interrogation method is special. He does not insult. He told me to give them my email address. I said I didn't have one.

Tell us about your interrogation sessions. Did interrogators really conduct any investigations? Were their questions about your work?

The first night we were taken to 209, the interrogation started immediately. Javad, Narges, my sister and I were interrogated in separate rooms. I could hear my husband's voice. For thirty-four days, I just argued with my interrogator. He once said that I had been watched for ten days before my arrest and that I had been filmed since the day I was released after my arrest in 2009. The discussions became more ideological, and I thought it was just a pretentious curtain-raiser and the real interrogations were yet to start.

Alawi argued and talked about various issues, especially the organization, more than he asked questions. I did not even ask if my daughter and sister had been released. So, they concluded that they could not threaten or pressure me through my family. However, they could pressure my family through me. The interrogators had called my home. 'Do you know that your mother is going to be executed?' they had asked Narges, my daughter. The spirits of my family were shattered. My mother had gone to the judge and complained. It was natural for me to be under pressure when I called home and was informed of the strain on my family. I did not want to resist, so to speak, or not talk. But I was not aware of my rights, not really. They wanted to accuse me of *moharebeh*.

If they were not questioning you about anything specific, what do you think they were looking for and what did they want?

I told Judge Salavati in court that if I were released, I would not be politically active. Salavati told me to talk to the experts. Alawi came. He said if I did not take back what I said in court, I had to write it down and I had to be interviewed. Their next step was to make me speak out against the organization. I replied that my motivation for doing what I did during the six months of being politically active was that when I was young, my father was unjustly executed. I was only eleven, but it was a bitter experience. I told them that when they arrested me and took my husband and daughter to the cell, that same bitter experience took root in the mind of my little daughter, who was also eleven years old. I said that on the day they arrested me at my mother's house, I remembered how I had felt as a child. 'I was not your enemy, but you killed my father unjustly. I did what I did against the oppression that was done to me. When I was eleven years old, you executed my father. As well as arresting my mother, you arrested my sixteen-year-old brother for having just one political flier and sentenced him to five years in prison. He endured it for four years and was released with the pardon of Ayatollah Montazeri.' Years later, six months before my arrest, I had just made a few fliers. My goal was only to protest the atrocities committed against me and my family.

I had not really done anything for which they could have executed me or declared me a *Mohareb*. I said if I were going to do an interview, I would talk about everything from the beginning, from the 1980s and everything that had happened to me. On the same day, the interrogator had also called my twenty-one-year-old and eleven-year-old girls and had told them to meet him in the park. He was going to see them after talking to me. In the interrogation room, my eldest daughter called him. He said it was my daughter on the phone and handed it over to me. I talked to her. But then I didn't know what my daughter was thinking when she rang up. Alawi had replied: 'Let me first talk to your mother.'

My mother had noticed that the girls were meeting with Alawi and had not allowed the girls to go to the park alone. She had gone with them and talked to him before he could talk to the girls. She had objected to my year-long solitary confinement. In any case, it had led to a quarrel. So, Alawi had not spoken to my daughters.

The next day he came to the ward and said he had gone to talk to the girls, but my family hadn't allowed him to. Later I understood that my daughters were going to be interviewed and videotaped. They wanted to use my daughters as they saw fit after they interviewed me. But because of what happened, they didn't do this. From that day onwards, for several months, they said that my file was missing. They would tell my mother that my file was lost every time she went to the prosecutor's office to follow up on my case and trial.

This is how I was left in a state of uncertainty in solitary confinement. After a few months I requested a meeting with Mr Alawi. 'Where is my file?' I asked. 'I'm neither taken to court nor am I told anything about my case.' Mr Alawi complained about that day in the park and about my mother. He gave me a phone number and left. Anyway, after this meeting, they found my file.

Were you threatened?

When I was in Ward 209 the pressure on my family was greater than on me. I was repeatedly threatened with execution by Mr Alawi. During interrogation I once said that I wanted my family, especially my daughters, to be in court during my trial. 'No,' he said. 'Because your sentence is execution, and it is better not to have them there.' There was a lot of pressure on my family. My mother was used to it, but my daughters were young. They were very scared and anxious. My daughters kept saying, 'Mummy, we do not want the calamity that befell you to befall us as well.' It was exceedingly difficult for my children.

How familiar were you with your rights as a defendant?

I didn't know anything about my rights. I didn't have access to anyone, including a lawyer. I only saw the interrogators. I didn't even see legal officials. One Monday I was fasting, and they took me for interrogation. They put my case in front of me and said that I had to explain my activities and sign all my case papers. I sat down from morning till evening and signed all the papers and explained my activities. I didn't know if what I did was right. They said it was for the court and the judge.

Do you have anything else you would like to say about the solitary cell?

Despite all the hardships I tried to look at the cell as an opportunity, not as a tragedy. I learned things there that I couldn't learn anywhere else. When I entered the women's ward later, I wondered where I had found the arguments I made during the interrogations. I was completely detached from the outside environment. Well! One becomes introverted in these circumstances, and I feel I had turned inward too. I read the Qur'an out loud. Every day I read two pages with its translation. Being in a solitary cell, I studied the Qur'an fourteen times carefully and meaningfully over the course of a year. This factor had a tremendous effect on reinforcing my resistance. I lived and resisted according to my religious beliefs.

In my cell I tried not to think about freedom, the world outside and getting out of prison. The last day of my trial was 7 December 2014. I went back to my cell and the next day at ten-thirty in the morning they called me. I didn't know what would happen as I came out of the cell. They told me nothing, and then I entered another building: the women's ward. My fourteen months in solitary confinement had ended.

NAZANIN ZAGHARI-RATCLIFFE

Nazanin Zaghari-Ratcliffe (born in 1979, Tehran) is an Iranian-British citizen who came to Iran on 6 April 2016 for a two-week trip but was detained at the airport when leaving Iran.

Nazanin was with her 22-month-old daughter Gabrielle (Gisoo) when she was arrested. The authorities took Nazanin's young child from her at the airport and handed her over to Nazanin's parents. The authorities confiscated Nazanin's passport and arrested her on charges of espionage and participating in 'subversive activities against the Islamic Republic through cooperation with foreign institutes and companies'. She was sentenced to five years in prison and was transferred to solitary confinement in Kerman Prison. Later they transferred her to Evin Prison. Richard Ratcliffe, her husband, and the Thomson Reuters Foundation, his employer, denied the allegations against Nazanin.

Do you remember anything about the
moment you were arrested?

The first night of detention I didn't know where I was. I don't remember what happened or what I did. I was shocked. I didn't know what had happened. No one gave me any explanations. Nobody told me why they were treating me like that, why they took my child away from me or where I was. The next day I was taken to interrogation. It was only later that I found out that my interrogations had begun at this moment. I was transferred to Kerman Prison on the afternoon of my arrest.

How was Kerman Prison? Were you
in solitary confinement there?

Kerman Central Prison had about 420 female prisoners. And it only had one quarantine cell at the time when 420 women were confined in the rest of the prison. I was first taken there. This room had a heavy iron door with a large iron lock that was always locked, and a hatch was welded onto it. The area of the quarantine cell was about two by one metre. Inside the cell was a half-wall with a squat toilet on the floor behind it. Next to it was a sink and a rubbish bin. The room had a fan. There was no natural light. There was a powerful light bulb in the centre that never went out.

Could you hear anything outside the cell, and did you have any contact with the women prisoners there?

All day long I heard the voices of the 420 women through the cell door. Their voices echoed in my head, but I had no contact with them.

How was it in the cell?

The floor of the cell was stone. They gave me a dirty blanket to place under me and an inadequate blanket to throw over me. The weather was cool and I slept in my coat, jeans and jacket.

And the hygiene?

It was awful. I was lucky to get out of there in good health. We did not have good detergent. They gave me a disposable glass of liquid soap to wash the toilet, sink and my hands. Sometimes they would also give me descaling agent. I had liquid soap when I was alone. Things got worse when people were brought into quarantine to be there for a few days with me, because we couldn't observe hygiene. Imagine that – the toilet and the bathroom were in the same cell where we ate and slept.

Could you shower?

I was not allowed to shower. They would give me a pan and a bowl and tell me to wash myself in the toilet.

What was it like to be there?

I couldn't sleep a wink for the first week. My heart palpitated so hard that when I put my head on the blanket it felt like it would explode. I knew day from night by the light coming in from the sides of the fan blades on the window. I prayed when I heard the call to prayer and realized that it was morning. Then morning would slither to noon, and noon to night. Silence was imposed from ten in the evening. I couldn't sleep at night and by the sound of sparrows I knew it was dawn.

How was the food?

They brought us food three times a day: breakfast, lunch and dinner. I was given a bottle of water each time. If I asked for water any time other than these three times, they would say that it wasn't possible because I had already taken my ration.

The quality of the food was awful, and I ate only bread, cheese and jam. The weather had become warmer. The days were hot, and the nights were cool. The heat was stifling during the day because there was no air conditioning or cooling. The cell toilet smelled so horrible that the guards covered their noses with their hands when they came to distribute food. It was very offensive.

I became sick several times. I had trouble breathing in that muggy air. It was hard enough in that cell when you were alone. Being solitary in a cell was exceedingly difficult. But it was worse when they brought people to the cell. A few times they brought drug addicts. In that small cell with its dirty open toilet, it was hard to bear the presence of some addicts.

How were the interrogations?

The interrogation started from the first day. In the first week I was interrogated every day. In the second week it was four times, and then it was three times a week. I was not taken outside the cell except during interrogation hours and I was never granted the right to be out in the fresh air. When I was in Kerman, I lost seven kilos.

How was the meeting with your family?

During the six days I was in Kerman I had only one meeting with my family. On the thirty-first day of my detention the meeting was in a guest house. I met my mother and father, Gisoo (my daughter) and my sister there. After the meeting I felt awful. Gisoo had changed. She had teethed. She didn't recognize me. I didn't recognize her either when I first saw her. When they came in, she was in my father's arms. I was so weak that I could not stand. She clung to me and didn't move at all for a few minutes. She looked at my mum and then at me. I felt like her face had changed during the forty days I hadn't seen her. Her canine teeth had come through, her hair was longer and she was taller. The interrogator had brought her a doll. Her first birthday was two weeks later. Gisoo was incredibly happy to see the doll. The interrogator pointed out that the room was wired and watched by a camera, and we were only allowed to talk about our family.

Were you allowed to make phone calls to your family?
There was no set schedule for phone calls. Everything depended on the interrogators' satisfaction with my interrogation. If they were satisfied, they would give me permission to make a call. If not, they would not allow it. They allowed it every day for the first week, but not after that.

How did you endure the pressure of the interrogations?
The interrogators threatened that I would receive a heavy sentence unless I confessed to espionage. They said that I did not know my husband and that he was a spy, and that he had lied about where he worked. I told them about my husband's emails that were sent from the company where he worked, but they would not accept this.

There were days when they wanted me to say that my husband was a spy and that I worked for intelligence organizations, but I refused. My situation got worse. I was kept in solitary confinement for forty days and in the general ward of Kerman Prison for eighteen days. The interrogators threatened to send Gisoo to London if I did not cooperate. They kept telling me that I had lost my job and that if interrogation took too long my husband would leave me. I was very frustrated. They asked me to tell them about my friends and their work projects. I had not really slept for three weeks. I had not seen my child and I was under a lot of pressure. Sometimes I said things just because I was under pressure. Once the interrogator brought his iPad and showed me fragments of Richard's interview. I cried so much once that I fainted. One day during the interrogation, I felt so overwhelmed that I fell off the chair. Interrogations in Kerman always distressed me. I was so anxious. The attitude and demeanour of the interrogator there bothered me greatly. I was very afraid of him.

How was your mental state in Kerman?

I felt awful in Kerman. I cried. I shouted. I read the Qur'an a lot. Maybe I finished the Qur'an seven times. I talked to God, shouted and fainted. When I woke up, I saw a rosary in my hand, and I fell on the rug. I realized that I had been unconscious for a long time. Time did not pass in Kerman at all. It was enormously difficult to pass the time there. I have not had such experiences here in Evin. Days passed sluggishly and nights were the same. And then again, I was taken to interrogation. If the interrogator thought the interrogation went well, he would ask what my favourite food was and they would order it.

What was the atmosphere like in the interrogation room?

I was taken from the quarantine cell to the interrogation place, and we'd drive for about three to five minutes and then they blindfolded me and I could not see the rest of the way. We entered a place that was residential. It was a house where I could lower my blindfold when we entered. I had to take off my shoes and go in with socks. There was a gentleman inside the building who would open the door every time when we rang the bell. There was another person in another room doing the typing and translating. When we got to the interrogation room, I took off my blindfold and sat down to wait for the interrogator to come.

Sometimes I sat waiting for hours. When the interrogator came, I heard them put the camera on the stand. He put a leather bag in front of himself so that I could not see what he was writing. He had another device in a small bag, which he turned on to record audio and video. Once I saw its flash, blinking. I was blindfolded again when the interrogator came and did these preparations. When this was done, I would take off my blindfold and the interrogation would begin. During interrogations they brought tea and sometimes cakes.

What effects did the solitary cell in Kerman, especially being away from Gisoo, have on your mental state?

I was very anxious. I wondered what the future would look like. I always wondered why my baby, whom I had breastfed two weeks before, was taken away from me. In the morning, when I opened my eyes, I looked for Gisoo. I had a vision in which I removed her straight hair from her face as she slept.

I thought I was in a nightmare. I could not believe I had been separated from Gisoo. I missed her a lot. I missed bathing her, putting her to sleep. Now that I think about it, I don't remember what I exactly thought. There are many things from Kerman that I don't remember. The atmosphere in Kerman Prison was so suffocating that I wanted to forget it.

Gisoo and I had never been apart. I had only been away from her for one night, and now she was removed from my arms. I thought Gisoo was no doubt feverish now, in my absence. She always used to put her hand on my face, chest and hands, and I wondered what she would do, how she would eat and sleep without me. I was extremely anxious. I thought this would not last more than a day or two. I didn't know it would take so long. Three days after my arrest, three interrogators came to Kerman from Tehran. They asked different questions. Among other things, I was asked various questions about my personality, which surprised me. Then I was told to text my husband and tell him there had been a misunderstanding and I would be released on Saturday. I was also told to call my parents to say the same thing.

But on Saturday I was taken for interrogation again. You will not be released, the interrogator said, 'The opinion of the Ministry of Intelligence towards you was positive the other day and now it is negative.' I was furious and objected to what they were doing to my family and me. I was terribly worried. My heart would beat so fast that I trembled out of fear.

How much did solitary confinement increase your distress and anxiety?

A lot. The solitary cell gave me panic attacks. I'm claustrophobic. Being confined and alone in solitary was severe torture because I was so scared. I told the women guards that if they left the door just slightly open, I could see them and I would calm down. At least I slept, but they said it was the law that the door and the hatch had to remain shut. On top of the anxiety and fear, I also experienced nostalgia and depression. I was worried about Gisoo and Richard. I wondered what they were doing. For almost the first month I was in Kerman, no one knew where I was because when I called my family, they couldn't see the phone number and I was not allowed to talk to my family about where I was.

With all the distress, were you taken to a psychiatrist or to the prison clinic for your other illnesses?

I was not taken to the health centre. I am severely deficient in iron and vitamin D. I was in treatment when I was free, but in prison I was not even allowed to have my pills. In the cell, these conditions are aggravated because you are deprived of normal living conditions.

The solitary cell was very tough. There was a narrow slit on the hatch that was welded to the door. I tried to look through it and see the women guards in the office. I would call them or knock on the door. They snacked on seeds, drank tea and talked to each other but paid me no attention. When I knocked on my cell door, the prisoners knocked on their door locks, which meant 'shut up'. It was a kind of torture.

When you said that the situation was bad and you needed help, did they not pay attention?

Every time I said I was hungry and asked them to give me some bread and cheese, they did not answer. When I just wanted to get out of the cell for a few minutes, they would not answer.

How did you pass the time in the cell?

I could not exercise or do anything. I was so shocked that I could not even walk in the cell. I kept whispering to God to help me. I did not know what to do. There was a Qur'an in my cell that I read constantly. The atmosphere in the cell was scary. I couldn't even bear to look around. There was a steel rod welded into the floor, ten centimetres from the wall, which bothered me. I didn't know what it was until the prisoners they brought into the cell said that it was used to punish prisoners who were soon to be executed. They tied them to that rod. It was terrifying. I was very petrified. I thought about the many people who had spent their last night here and who had been tied to this bar. I felt like I could hear their voices. There was nothing in the cell but a toilet, a bucket, two blankets, a Qur'an and a copy of the book *Mafatih al-Jinan*.

How did you feel when you could talk to Gisoo on the phone?

The phone calls were very short. What effect could a three-minute call have? I wanted to talk much longer to Gisoo, but they wouldn't let me. I was devastated and could not believe it.

Did calling your family, bathing, eating, etc., change your mental and emotional state?

No, these things brought me no joy and didn't change or affect me in any way.

What exactly were the interrogators looking for?

They tried to induce me to say something that didn't exist. They said they had top-secret evidence that I worked for the British parliament and against Iran.

I was sure that was not the case, but they repeated it so much that I doubted myself when I returned to the cell. I asked myself, for instance, if there was any talk of Iran when I was at the British Foreign Office. Basically, my work projects were for other countries. I spent long hours in my cell wondering if the projects I had worked on had anything to do with Iran. Then I told myself that I was a hundred per cent sure that my projects had nothing to do with Iran, but after each interrogation I would review these cases over and over again. Despite my certainty, I still had doubts due to the interrogators' repeated insistence, and I reviewed everything again and again.

For a long time, I didn't remember things clearly. I thought for hours in the cell, but I could not even remember simple, everyday tasks. I could not remember the names of the projects on which I used to work every day. I was familiar with the names of the people they mentioned, but I could not remember who they were. I was interrogated for hours on ordinary and non-problematic issues that I had worked on for a long time. I dealt with such issues for forty-five days in the quarantine cell and eighteen days in the Kerman public ward.

The truth is that none of the issues alleged by the interrogators ever really existed. There was no big issue at all, but I was interrogated in vain for hours and days unendingly.

What happened after the sixty days in Kerman?
Were you transferred to solitary confinement again?

I was transferred to Tehran on 7 June 2016. I was told I would be released. I called my mother and told her I did not trust the interrogators. I told her that they might not release me but just transfer me to another prison.

In Kerman, I was taken to a building that belonged to the IRGC. We entered a room with a row of chairs around. I noticed a camera recorder. I was supposed to be transferred. I said, 'Why have you brought me here?' They said that someone was coming to see me. I was given a very substantial and sophisticated lunch, but I said I would not eat. The camera was on to film me eating a hearty meal. While in quarantine, sometimes they wouldn't even give me bread and cheese. I remember that day I got angry and involuntarily shouted, 'You are all the same!' One of them started yelling at me. I insisted that they call my interrogator to come so I could talk to him. I asked them to turn off the camera, but they did not. Eventually, I was transferred to Tehran, to another ward of the Revolutionary Guards called 2A.

I was taken to Tehran by flight. They took me part of the way to the prison in one car. Then they changed the car and I asked the driver to let me at least call my mother and tell her I would not be coming home, but the driver said that I had to stay with them that night so that the judge on duty at the courthouse could talk to me and then I would be released. I talked to the Tehran interrogator on the phone. 'Who told you that you are free?' He told me. 'You have only been transferred from Kerman to Tehran.'

They asked me to give my family's number so that they could phone my parents themselves, but they didn't. Seven days later, I called my family and told them that I had been transferred to Tehran.

Where did you go?

I was taken to the cells of Security Ward 2A, which belong to the Revolutionary Guards. This cell was smaller and had no windows. There was a white light on the ceiling. The toilet was inside the cell and it was carpeted. I had three blankets. I felt strangely homesick in Kerman. I did not feel this way in Tehran. I felt that Tehran was my city, as this was where my family lived.

Did you have any open-air hours?

Twice a day for half an hour, in the morning and in the evening.

How were the phone calls and meetings with family?

I didn't have phone calls on the first days. I made a phone call when I was being transferred to Tehran, two months after I was arrested. On the Sunday after I was transferred to Tehran, Mr Hajiloo, the prosecutor's assistant, came to my cell and let me call my family. I introduced myself. He asked me about the whole process, wrote detailed notes, and then he asked if I had seen my daughter. After two hours he allowed me to make a phone call. He made an appointment for me to see my family the next day. I was permitted to have a meeting with my family every two weeks.

How was your first meeting with Gisoo and your parents?

Eight days after coming to Tehran and meeting with Mr Hajiloo I was allowed to see Gisoo. Our second meeting took place on the seventieth day of my detention. The second meeting was better than the first one because it was in Tehran and I felt closer to my family. Kerman Prison was very tough, and I felt bitter. My family had travelled all that distance, at great expense, just to bring my little daughter to visit me. All of this worried me a lot.

On the day of the meeting in Tehran, my mother brought me fruit. She had prepared food for me. Eating the food my mother had made felt very good after all that time. The meeting room had a carpet. In meetings, Gisoo would bring toys and we would play together. This sincere family atmosphere felt good. Gisoo had accepted that her mother lived in a room and she said this repeatedly. She cried when she had to leave, and I was very upset. When I returned to my cell, I could smell Gisoo's scent on my body and it was painful. When Gisoo asked me to go to Grandma's house, I didn't know what to say. I was exasperated. Every time she cried goodbye, I would break down. The interrogators were present in the meeting room. When saying goodbye, I wanted to go ahead and tie her shoes for her, but they wouldn't let me and I had to leave her.

How was the cell's atmosphere?

When I was taken to Ward 2A, there were a lot of women who had been imprisoned for sex work and I was with them sometimes. We did not have a TV for the first ten days but then they gave us one. At first, I did not have books and newspapers, but about two and a half months later I could receive books sent by my friends through my family. It felt great to receive books. The thought that my friends and Rebecca (my sister-in-law) had sent me books delighted me. Initially they did not give me newspapers. When only a few of us were left in Ward 2A and I went to Homa's[1] cell, I saw a lot of newspapers there. After some time, they'd bring a newspaper every day, unless there was important news that they did not want us to know.

1 Homa Hoodfar is a Canadian-Iranian academic who researches Muslim women and the veil. She was detained in Iran in 2016 for over a hundred days.

What was the food situation like in 2A?

Except for Ramadan, when the food was good, the quality of the food was poor. For a few months, I couldn't buy anything and had to eat the food they gave me. Some of the prisoners could make a shopping list to order. For example, they would order biscuits, dates, milk, etc., but I was not allowed to make a shopping list for five months. I often ate tahini and bread. Sometimes I cried, 'God, you've imprisoned me, at least give me good food!' I cried from hunger. The food for the guards was different from ours and was of better quality. I went on a hunger strike. I only drank water and milk. Once I ate a date and a digestive biscuit. Because I was so sick, they let my family visit me on the sixth day. My mother suddenly became ill and fainted. Gisoo's heart was beating like a sparrow. She kept saying, 'Granny fell'. They kicked us out of the meeting room and immediately brought me a bowl of broth and said, 'You'll not go out until you eat this bowl of broth.' I did not comply. But my parents insisted that I eat, and I saw that my mother was feeling worse. So, I had to eat the broth. The interrogator promised to fix the food problem. At that time, Afarin[2] and I were the only ones in Ward 2A. The interrogator promised that Afarin and I would be together. The next morning, she was brought to my cell. They also brought me food. This led to a slight improvement in our food.

---

2 Afarin Neyssari is an Iranian-American architect. For two years she and her husband were held in Evin Prison without trial, being released in 2018.

How was your medical treatment?

We did not receive any medical treatment. My right hand had been numb for a long time and my neck hurt a lot. I could not turn it left or right. I was extremely tired. I became so tired after just a few minutes' walking that I could not continue. My heart would palpitate so hard. I had nausea and they regularly gave me anti-emetics, but they didn't take special care of me. They said it was a virus and that I had to rest and drink boiled water.

What happened with your iron and vitamin D deficiency?

The physician of the prison's health centre prescribed iron pills. I had hair loss. I asked them to allow my family to bring me the pills, but the interrogators wouldn't allow it. They brought zinc pills themselves and gave them to me.

For how long did you not see yourself in the mirror? How did you react when you saw your face?

I did not see myself at all in the quarantine cell of Kerman for forty-five days. I saw how I looked in the mirror in the public ward and I remember how sad and emotional it made me. In 2A there was no mirror at all, so I couldn't see my reflection.

After five months, one of my roommates wanted to trim her eyebrows and asked for a mirror. That's when I looked at myself. Some things were very annoying, that you didn't know what you looked like, for instance, or how different your face had become. You couldn't remember what you used to look like before and how different you were now. It was a strange feeling. There was something else that irritated me a lot. Throughout all those nine months I drank tea from a plastic cup. I ate without a fork and with a plastic spoon. Eating with plastic utensils was so irritating.

Did you sleep better?

Never. I did not sleep. And if I did, it was as if I hadn't rested. There was no proper place to sleep. I put a military blanket under my head instead of a pillow and another under me and I pulled one over me.

How were your clothes in the cell?

From the very beginning they took my clothes in 2A and gave me a loose pink coat and trousers made of plastic. When we wanted to leave the cell, we wore a chador and a mask and were blindfolded.

What was the atmosphere like during the interrogations in 2A?

In Tehran, a young man interrogated me who knew English and sometimes spoke English to me. He knew that I loved dates and Nescafé. Sometimes he would send me food. In general, the attitude of the interrogators was better in Tehran. But once during interrogation one of the interrogators wanted to digress. He started asking questions about porn websites, and about Richard – questions that had nothing to do with my case and I was not comfortable answering them. I was often interrogated in a dark room. There was a pane of mirror glass in front of me as I sat. The interrogators sat behind the glass. On the interrogators' side, there was also a window facing the terrace for those who wanted to smoke. I could not see them, but I just heard their voices. On my side there was an office chair and a desk.

Did this atmosphere bother you?

It does not feel good to talk to someone you can't see, but the fact is that I felt comfortable not seeing the faces of my interrogators. In Kerman, it bothered me to see the interrogators.

During interrogations in that atmosphere, I preferred not to see my interrogator. Seeing the interrogator was distressing. It was a strange feeling that I could not explain. The older interrogator in Tehran did not allow me to call Richard, but the younger one did. And then he started asking inappropriate and irrelevant questions. Back then, when he tried to provide me with some of the things I longed for, like Nescafé, I'd thought he understood me.

How did you feel in the cell in 2A?

I missed Gisoo very much and I felt depressed. The fact is that I felt better because I had entered Tehran. Occasionally I talked to Richard for half an hour and saw Gisoo more often, but it made me miss her even more. The interrogator loved her and wanted to hug her. Once when he hugged Gisoo during the meeting, I wanted to take Gisoo from his arms and beat him. I had gone through a difficult period. It can't really be described. I had many ups and downs. Near my birthday, when they let me out for some fresh air, I walked and talked to God. I said 'God, let me go, God forgive me', and so on. My thoughts were not under my control. It was as if I was not on my own. It was as if I was doing things, I knew I could not do. I often spoke loudly and recited prayers. Even though I knew I would not be released, I hoped it would not last. One day they told Afarin to pack up and go. I felt so bad. My heart started to pound. Being alone was awfully hard for me. From that night on, they some-times left the cell door open. They said they knew I was innocent. I knew they understood that I felt lonely. Sometimes they brought me their own food. Late at night, sometimes one of them would come and talk to me for hours. I felt they pitied me, but at the end of the day I was all alone, even with these people.

MAHVASH SHAHRIARI

Mahvash Shahriari (born in 1952 in Zavareh District, Ardestan County, Isfahan Province) was arrested in Mashhad on 5 March 2008 and sentenced to twenty years in prison. On 18 September 2017 she was released after the application of Article 134.

When she was ten years old, Mahvash moved to Tehran with her family. After finishing high school she studied education at university. She taught in national schools at the same time. Later she was hired by the Ministry of Education and worked as a school teacher and principal in deprived areas and the southern suburbs of Tehran.

Following the 1979 Revolution and then the 1980–83 Cultural Revolution, Mahvash was expelled from the Department of Education for believing in what the govern-ment called the 'errant Bahá'í sect' and was no longer allowed to be employed by any government organization. She was also barred from continuing university education and stayed at home for a while. At the same time, her husband's work and property were confiscated by the government.

Mahvash later engaged in educational services in the Bahá'í community of Iran, and co-founded the Institute of Higher Education, which was established to compensate to some degree for the deprivation of the Bahá'í youth of Iran, namely their being barred from attending university.

She was elected a member of the ad hoc group of the Yaran in 2006, and, along with six other members of the group, ran the affairs of the Bahá'í community in Iran. Mahvash was the secretary of this delegation until her arrest.

When was your first solitary cell experience?

On the morning of 25 May 2005, the day my daughter's wedding was to be held, six intelligence agents raided our house at six o'clock in the morning. After searching our house for about five or six hours, in addition to gathering and taking various books, my writings, and anything that could be interpreted as a symbol of our religion, they arrested me and transferred me to Ward 209 of Evin. For the next thirty-four days, I experienced solitary confinement.

Did you not receive a sentence during this period?

No, I was released on bail.

Did you continue your work at the Bahá'í Educational Institute after your arrest?

Yes, of course, I continued for as long as I was a member of the Yaran committee.

After your second arrest, did they put you in solitary confinement?

Yes, on 6 March 2008, following a phone call, I travelled to Mashhad to answer some questions posed by the Khorasan Razavi Intelligence Office. I was asked to go to the Mashhad Revolutionary Court, but I was arrested on my arrival by unknown agents, and I was blindfolded and taken some-where. There was a hasty interrogation, and I was taken to the Revolutionary Court at night, where I was arraigned on a minor matter. At the same court hearing, the judge set a bail of ten million tomans[1] and said that I could be released imme-diately on bail, but for about three months they prevented my family from being informed about the bail, and I was not even allowed to call my family to inform them.

I endured about three months of strict detention with lengthy and intense interrogations. I was in the solitary confinement cell of Vakilabad Public Prison, called Sagduni;[2]

1 One toman was equivalent to ten rials. Ten million tomans would be equivalent to roughly $2,360. Subsequently, the toman has become the official currency of Iran and is now equal to 10,000 rials.
2 Sagduni means a place where dogs are kept, but not necessarily a kennel. It's used to humiliate prisoners.

the quarantine cell of Vakilabad Prison; and in the public ward for the punishment of internal crimes, which was separated from the main area of the prison. No one there was allowed to contact the other prisoners. Prolonged solitary confinement and intense interrogation, along with being away from and out of touch with my family and being constantly threatened with harm to my community and my family caused a number of problems. I had respiratory problems, palpitations, insomnia and restlessness. Being deprived of meetings with my family and the right to make phone calls, which are normally allowed in Security Ward 209, made the situation more difficult for me. One of the tactics to demoralize me was to take me to the Revolutionary Court twice, along with many prisoners who were chained by both their hands and feet. To make matters worse, the police mistreated us all and specifically me. The interrogations, on the other hand, did not involve any charges against me except on the first day. In this way they extended my detention despite its illegality.

What was the hardest part of this solitary confinement for you?

Unscrupulous interrogations that were not limited to any rules and regulations and covered all personal and public affairs of our society, and the feeling of homelessness in a city that was far away from my family. I was all alone. There were no female prisoners in this ward. They did not have a female officer, and for this reason they sometimes sent me to the isolated parts of Vakilabad Prison during religious holidays. I must say that this kind of solitude was so difficult that I preferred Sagduni to the public prison, because I knew that I was in a female environment and that there were other women prisoners nearby.

How did the detention in Mashhad end?

After eighty-two days I was finally transferred to Tehran with two intelligence agents. I was immediately taken to the Revolutionary Court, where the judge arraigned me with new charges and extended my detention for fifteen days. This time I was arrested as the secretary of the Yaran committee. This detention lasted ten years.

How and where did you spend the first night in Mashhad?

It was midnight when I returned from the Revolutionary Court of Mashhad to Vakilabad Prison and after a long admission procedure, I was sent to quarantine.

What was that like?

It was very painful and unbelievable for me, because I did not expect it and didn't know anything about it: a small room with three bunk beds, with the ward lawyer and two others.

From this room we entered the main hall with, I think, ten three-storey beds that were full and many people who were on the floor. I was fasting and I was very tired and cold. No one gave me a blanket or anything else, and I was not told where to sleep and what to do. I stood shaking at the entrance. Several people looked at me in amazement from the beds, but I stood still and wondered what to do. A woman was lying on the floor with a very dirty blanket over her. I sat down quietly. My foot became stiff from the cold. I thought of gently slipping the tip of my toes under the woman's blanket. She noticed and pulled her blanket away. In short, I did not sleep that night and I shivered and waited for the morning.

It was very early when I was called. The same two agents came again. They were waiting for me at the police station. They took their weapons from the station and we went out. Blindfolded, I felt we went a long way. I was taken to the previous cell, then I was immediately taken to the interrogation room by an old man who was usually there. The interrogation lasted until night-time and I was transferred to the quarantine of the public ward the same night. It took them so long to transfer me that I had become hungry, but they wouldn't let me eat anything.

You mentioned a place called Sagduni.
Where was this place and how was it?

This cell was in Vakilabad Prison. In the prison toilet and baths, there was a small, low door with a very small lattice glasswork in it. From there we entered a small corridor with two or three cells. They took me to a very small and dirty cell which stank. It had no natural light, with an uncovered Iranian toilet in the corner, contaminated with dead and living beetles. It had a low ceiling whose corner had collapsed. When they unlocked the chains and locks to take me inside, several young girls ran up behind the officers and each of them asked me 'What do you need, prisoner?'

Two of them pulled a piece of black carpet from the next-door cell into the second cell they had planned for me. Someone threw an old magazine on the carpet. They gave me two dirty blankets, a bottle of boiled water and some dry tea. They also put some sugar cubes in my hand.

I was so shocked that I did not know how to respond. I wondered how many days I had to be there and how I could survive.

I was hungry and tired. I was cold. There was no air to breathe. The stench of the toilet, the tiredness and anxiety of the interrogations, the uncertainty and the long transferral processes worked together to intensify the physical and mental pressure. When the officers and girls left, I wanted to sit down, warm myself up first and then drink some tea. I had already put some sugar cubes in my mouth when I heard a moaning and screaming sound coming from the next cell.

A woman was in there, and now she thought she had found someone in the same painful situation. She was crying. She cried and cursed. She begged me and said, 'Give me anything you might have, a painkiller, a cigarette.' I immediately talked to her and tried to calm her down. Behind the window, the kind girls were still standing and shouting. 'Hey you in the solitary cell! What do you need us to bring you in the morning?' 'Books and magazines,' I told them, 'Whatever there is.'

I did not know that this cell really didn't have the light you needed to read or the air you needed to breathe.

At first, I didn't know how to sleep on the floor next to that dirty toilet, on that dirty carpet and under those stinking old blankets. The intensity of the cold and fatigue made me accept the situation and I sat on the carpet. I drank some of that tea from the bottle. Now I was warm and while I was calming down, the memory of Tehran's dungeons at the time of Bahá'u'lláh increased my strength. I felt as though I was in the dungeon where Bahá'u'lláh had once been a long time ago, in the mud and in chains for a long time. It seemed as if everything I had read in history about Bahá'u'lláh was now happening before my eyes, inspiring and strengthening me spiritually. I gently pulled the blanket over me, put the already cooled bottle aside and slept with my back to the stinking toilet. It was here that a truth was revealed to me. I said to myself that they wanted to humiliate and degrade me with what they did to me, but it would never happen. I said to myself, this is a spiritual experience for me. I remembered

Nietzsche's aphorism: 'What doesn't kill you makes you stronger.'

I decided to return home stronger. Early the next morning the doors opened with the clatter of locks and chains and I was handed over to the officers through administrative procedures and a relatively long journey, and once again I was sat in the interrogation chair.

Tell us about the interrogations.

The interrogation continued from morning till night, long and detailed. But I tried my best to answer only the questions related to my accusations. To the questions that had nothing to do with the accusations I either did not answer at all or I answered incompletely and incomprehensibly. I objected to the blindfold. So, they would sit me on a chair for hours on end and leave. They gave me very thick and wide blindfolds so that I could not even see the ground under my feet, and the old man kept saying: 'Be careful not to fall.'

Have you experienced other types of cells as well?

Yes. After Sagduni in the intelligence office, I was moved to a relatively larger room with a few blankets in the corner as a kind of a mattress. There was a cream-coloured blanket on the floor. The toilet had a shower that was separated from the cell by a door, so there was the same nasty smell in the room. The first thing I did was wash the door and its wall.

Unfortunately, the strong smell did not dissipate. There was a hatch on the wall just below the ceiling that provided light to the cell.

The window was not visible, and the light was very dim, but at dawn I heard a bird singing, which I really enjoyed. It was a sign of life for me. For the first three days my transfer was arranged in a way that I couldn't have lunch or dinner. One night when I finally reached the last bunk in quarantine, I saw a piece of dry bread on the bed, by the pipe. I was so hungry that I picked it up, looked at it hesitantly, lay down and ate it and felt a little better. It was a cold night, and I couldn't stop shivering. It finally occurred to me to pull the edge of the heavy dry carpet over me. But then I saw that there was a hatch under the ceiling next to my head and the wind was coming through it. I couldn't do anything. I thought I would freeze.

What was it like to be in solitary confinement?

A solitary confinement cell is not just a small, cramped, dark, lifeless cell. During this period, the pressure on the accused is constantly increasing, with heavy and intense interrogations, threats, insults, a sense of impending danger to one's family and others, not knowing about one's family, being unaware of their plans for you, your family and your community. You are making important decisions with every question that you must answer. In addition, they are constantly bluffing, swearing, shouting and lying to wear you out and make you obedient.

Prolonged solitary confinement has serious physical and psychological costs. Isolation gradually numbs your senses and disturbs your mental balance. You can't make any plans, and this is combined with confusing and sometimes intrusive thoughts, and the absence of sensory stimuli such as light, colour, sound, pleasant scents, touch and even a simple, neutral look. There is also the bad sleep, insomnia and loss of weight because of disrupted eating habits. I lost about twenty kilos in a few months.

What were you threatened with?

The most difficult threat was when the interrogator told me that my son came to Mashhad twice a week and that it was dangerous because there might be an accident on the way; or when he said that my husband wouldn't come to Mashhad because if he came, he would be arrested and executed immediately for apostasy. 'You will not leave here alive,' the interrogator would always say. There were many threats like this.

I believed them, of course, in Ward 209, when the case was completely different and the indictment was the death penalty – it was no longer just a threat. He also said that Mr Tavakoli – another member of the Yaran committee – was in a cell there, which was a lie. 'Your poor husband is in the hospital,' he would say. 'Was he ill? We didn't intend it to be your last farewell.' I believed that something bad had happened to my husband. And this was really disturbing to me, given my complete lack of information about my family and colleagues.

What was the food like?

Maybe the quality of food was not bad, but for other reasons it could not be eaten. When I was in the cell, I could hear the iron wheels of the food cart. I would get up and walk to the door to grab the old, broken aluminium bowl from the old man as he handed it over to me through the hatch at the bottom of the door. The teacup was an old red plastic cup – the tea smelled of plastic. I was frustrated by their disrespectful behaviour. Most of my food remained untouched. That is why I lost so much weight. I think I became sick because I often shivered, and at night I would sweat and change the blanket. I took a shower every night to feel a little better. I washed my clothes as much as possible and spread them on the floor on my chador to dry.

Were you taken out for fresh air?

It was so quick. If the interrogators saw fit, I would be taken out for a few minutes. I could just take three steps across, but at least it was not as putrid and depressing as that cell.

You said they didn't have a female agent. Weren't you annoyed?

Of course I was annoyed. I didn't feel safe because the cell only opened from the outside. Once the old man suddenly opened the door, I jumped up and protested. While I was in the cell, sometimes a young girl who was apparently an employee would hastily come in and then leave. There were nights when an old woman came and slept behind the door, in the corridor. She said she was a retired prison guard, and she was asked to come at night to take care of me. She said she came only for God's sake. In the first days I was fasting, and I told her. She was a kind woman. During interrogation, she brought me a cup of tea when it was iftar[3] time. The interrogator did not say anything on the first day, but on the second day he protested. 'What is this?' he asked. 'This woman is fasting,' she replied. 'It's iftar time.' The interrogator did not allow it and I heard the kind old woman say, 'I came for God's sake, not for your sake . . .'

I didn't feel well at all. I didn't trust them, and this was probably one of the causes of my poor sleep in Mashhad. To all this I must add the feeling of homesickness. In Mashhad, I felt so far away from my family, my home and my city!

---

3 Iftar is the meal with which Muslims break their fast in Ramadan.

What did you do alone in solitary confinement?

I would clean the toilet and the carpet in the cell and take a shower. I'd make prayers and supplications for a very long time. I walked around the room again and again, and recited aloud the poems and texts I had memorized. I remember making a schedule to think. For example, I thought about my interrogations and I even had some kind reflections about them. I thought about my home and family. I thought about my colleagues, my friends and so on. I tried to avoid thinking about unsettling things so that I wouldn't lose control of my thoughts.

Talking to the guard, however briefly, was good for me. Clearly, I needed someone to talk to. I even remember that I told myself to think of it as teaching a class. I taught a subject from a management course. I practised in order to keep my mind active.

Can you tell us about complications caused by solitary confinement?

Humans are social beings – in other words, talking animals. That is, social communication is a natural human need. I faced these complications: fear of a closed environment, fear of endangering the interests of an oppressed community, fear of dangers to one's family and others, fear of instigating a wave of aggression and attacks on one's community, fear of prolonging the detention period, physical weakness, continuous weight loss, insomnia and bad sleep, reviewing the interrogator's questions and behaviour, reviewing one's own answers and thinking of a new strategy. I would like to emphasize again that living in an unknown environment in absolute silence, an environment that, regardless of how familiar it becomes, is an environment of hostility and conflict, and you know you are a prisoner of a system that does not accept anything less than your death and the death of your beloved community, all this leads to very destructive consequences on your soul and body.

How did the public ward compare with the intelligence ward in Mashhad?

I was never free in the Mashhad public ward and was kept in solitary confinement, but I still preferred it and waited to be transferred there. Although my first experience was in the company of various murderers, thieves and criminals, in practice I realized I was not afraid of them. They were very compassionate, waiting for me and asking me how I was doing when I arrived, explaining my situation and comforting me. In my presence, they were respectful and did not behave inappropriately. I thought that I had never dreamed of being the companion of such people before, let alone that I would look forward to seeing them. But I eagerly awaited seeing them.

When did the interrogations end?

I was interrogated until one or two days before my transfer
to Tehran.

How were you taken to Tehran?

One morning they finally called me and said that I was being
transferred to Evin Prison. They said they had taken money
from my purse to buy a plane ticket. I was transferred to
Tehran with two intelligence agents. They handed me over
to two other agents, along with two envelopes obviously
constituting my file.

How did you feel in Tehran?

I wanted to fly out of happiness. I thought I had come home
and been released. I was so happy that I talked to the driver,
who was a young and well-tempered man, all the way to the
Revolutionary Court and then from there to the prison.

A man was sitting next to me in the back seat, writing fast.
I thought he was writing what I said, and I wondered why
he didn't record it. Maybe he did.

Where did they take you?

Ward 209 of Evin Prison.

What happened there?

After the usual admission process, I was transferred to cell 215, the smallest cell in Corridor Two. The cell was so small that I thought it was impossible to breathe and live in such a place. The cell had little light. There was a vent under the roof, but there was a large, noisy air conditioner on the ceiling in front of the vent, and a small steel sink and a small steel toilet that could no longer be used.

But did you still feel glad to be in Tehran?

Not any more. Do you know what happened? As I was going down the corridor, from under the blindfold I saw a pair of brown shoes behind the first cell's door. I recognized the shoes. They were Fariba's shoes.[4] Oh, everything was all clear to me now; the purpose behind the ill-treatment and the reason why the judge of the Revolutionary Court in Tehran asked me if I had heard of my colleagues. My heart sank and I wanted to be sure. Under the pretext of going to the bathroom, I went back to Corridor One and checked the shoes again. Yes, it was her. Fariba was there, meaning that my other colleagues had also been arrested. Everything was over and I knew that they had decided to capitalize on the opportunity to deal with our organization.

4 Fariba Kamalabadi belonged to the Friends in Iran, and was arrested with the other six members in 2008. She was imprisoned for nine and a half years. Her father had also been persecuted by the state.

What happened next?

My interrogations began on the day after I arrived, on 28 May. Now I was arraigned on the charge of being the secretary of the Yaran committee, and as I was in Tehran, I had to answer other questions too.

After all the interrogations in Mashhad, what did they want from you now? Were they really looking for something?

Not at all. The first series of interrogation questions in 209 were fully engineered and calculated. In fact, it was set up only to prove allegations they had made up. In other words, it was just to find something to use as a pretext so that they could falsely charge me. They were clearly seeking to prove the charges required to obtain a death sentence. For example, they wanted to prove the accusation that our organization had ties to foreign countries. So, the interrogators attached copies of our correspondence with the Universal House of Justice, which is the Bahá'í International Centre and has nothing to do with any government, and wanted us to confess that these were documents proving our cooperation with other governments.

Did you accept these allegations?

Of course not. We have never been in contact with any government, but we have been in contact with the Universal

House of Justice, which is the Bahá'í World Centre, only regarding matters concerning the Bahá'í s of Iran, and the two are quite different. They wanted to use our correspondence with the Bahá'í World Centre and turn the issue upside down and use that information as they desired.

How long were you confined in 209?

Two years and three months. I was in the solitary confinement cell for a total of seven months.

How were the solitary confinement cells in 209 and Mashhad different?

The solitary confinement cell in 209 was of course better. I felt closer to my family there and knew my colleagues were also there. Although I had thousands of questions, all of which went unanswered, it seemed that I was no longer the only person responsible for our organization. And the interrogations were different. Although I had another interrogation period which was full of insults and unscrupulous behaviour, at least the cell was in a ward and many people were by my side.

Were you allowed to make phone calls or meet your family?

Sometimes a short phone call was permitted in the presence of the interrogator. After my solitary confinement had ended, we had family visits every fifteen days supervised by the interrogator, and after a while we had regular meetings.

What physical and psychological effects has solitary confinement had on you?

It is still too early to answer this question because I am still in prison and haven't been examined by a doctor, but in Mashhad I suffered from shortness of breath and heart palpitations. In Ward 209, my weight loss continued. I developed advanced osteoporosis; I got hyperlipidaemia because of anxiety. I also suffered from a less frequently mentioned complication: memory impairment.

After my three-stage interrogation period was over, especially when I wanted to check the interrogations and events with Fariba, I realized that I had lost the thread and that my memory had not yet been restored. Inactivity naturally leads to depression and burnout. Although I used to work out in the morning and evening for up to three hours every day, I didn't live a normal life. We did not have enough light in the cell. We did not have enough mobility. We did not have enough fruit and vegetables, and sometimes didn't have any at all. Our food was neither healthy nor sufficient. We did not have a proper bed and slept on military blankets and carpets for years, which resulted in bedsores, pelvic joint pain and wear, backache and fatigue. Moreover, the lack of necessary communication and routine discussions, especially for me, who has been teaching and learning in educational institutions for many years, has caused serious mental and emotional damage. I have described these clearly in my poems.

Has there been any other emotional or psychological damage?

Of course. Separation from my husband and children, from my father who was old and always came to visit me, from my sister, from my brother who travelled all the way to visit me for years and had to cope with the anxiety. These experiences were not easy for me. I didn't even understand the dimensions of this isolation and unfortunately years later I saw the complications resulting from it. To be isolated from the passage of time, to be isolated from society, to be removed from the natural cycle of life, and to be thrown into a corner out of reach, is the definition of solitary confinement.

When and how did you find out about the physical and mental damage?

When I saw my family in Tehran after almost seven months, I felt strange. When they'd announced that I was meeting my family, I was frozen and my mind was stagnant. I must say I was totally absent-minded. I felt nothing. I was taken to the lawyers' meeting place, which was later changed to the place where sentences were pronounced. The interrogator was there too, sitting by the tall windows that opened onto the wooded area of the prison. I sat down as well. I was looking at the outside while wearing a chador and very large plastic men's slippers. I had no excitement or sense of joy. There seemed to be no ideas in my head at all. My mind was thoughtless and emotionless, still and stagnant. I looked at the tall trees and the green grass and the narrow path that came towards us. Then I saw some men and women coming along that narrow path. I stared at them and the interrogator monitored my reactions. As they approached, I recognized my sweet daughter, Negar, who was speeding towards our building ahead of everyone. I saw my dear son, Foroud, who had come to Mashhad twelve times in three months. My husband was with them.

There was something in me like a barrier that stopped the flow of feelings and thoughts. Every sensation felt suppressed. Neither my heart nor my brain reacted. Finally, they arrived. I hugged my son and put my mouth close to his ear for a long time and calmly told him, 'Honey, don't trust this judge of Mashhad. Because the judge once implied to me that you could have an "accident" on your commute.'

'Mama, Mashhad is over,' he said, 'you have nothing to do with Mashhad any more and I will not go to Mashhad again.'

I did not realize there was a time limit, and that my husband and daughter were waiting. I remember saying nothing. I just wanted to touch them and be touched by them and take in their perfume in the depths of my soul and store it in my soul for the rest of my life. Later I would ask myself what had happened to me that I was in such a state. Then I had another bitter experience. After several months I became sick and was taken to a health centre outside 209, the main health centre of Evin Prison. We had to take the elevator to the other floor. It was me and the woman who was the head of the women's ward. Suddenly my eyes set on the mirror in the elevator, and I saw someone I did not know. I stared at her and wondered who she was. I asked myself if there was anyone other than her and me. I looked around and saw that there were only the two of us. So, was that yellow, skinny, emaciated woman with white hair and untrimmed eyebrows, me? I immediately felt bad that I hadn't recognized myself.

How do you feel about prison now, after almost ten years?

I have two contradictory emotions: the feeling of physical exhaustion and fatigue from oppression and cruelty, and a strong spiritual conviction, a sense of love for all human beings and a firm faith in them. Also, the feeling of being away from my family and friends, and the joy of finding valuable friends in prison and gaining unique experiences that would not have been possible without enduring all this suffering. In other words, there is this feeling of isolation from society and loneliness in prison, and there is an opposite feeling of having experienced a difficult but meaningful collective life. The experience of prison is long, special and unique: a life steeped in suffering, deprivation and loneliness. It is an experience of carrying the burden of injustice and enduring bitter and naked immorality. Life in prison is based on the denial of all natural and human needs, but at the same time it opens the doors of poetry, thought and meaning in the heart and soul. It's a way of achieving belief and certainty in the ultimate victory of truth; it's the ascetic experience of finding *Haqq al-Yaqin*.[5] Life in prison, if it is to end with discovering a steadfast and noble faith, makes you more stable and prouder than before.

I would like to thank all those who have supported and defended me during these ten years. I thank my dear compatriots inside Iran, my lawyers who paid a heavy price for defending me, and all the organizations, groups and human rights associations, in particular PEN International.

5 'For, verily, it is truth absolute', Quran 69:9-12. The term 'truth absolute' refers also to a concept in Islamic mysticism, a stage in which a Sufi has no doubt in the truthfulness of God.

HENGAMEH SHAHIDI

Hengameh Shahidi (born in 1975) is a journalist and a press and women's rights activist.

She has been arrested several times, the first lasting from July to November 2009, following the events surrounding the presidential election. In March 2010 she was sentenced to six years in prison on charges of 'gathering and colluding with intent to harm state security' and 'insulting the head of state'. She was arrested again in July 2016, and again in March 2017 and released in September of the same year. In June 2018, she was arrested once more, and that December, in Branch 15 of the Revolutionary Court, Judge Salavati sentenced her to twelve years and nine months in prison. She was also banned for two years from joining any political organization and from partaking in any online or media activities.

Hengameh's daughter, Parmis, has endured much suffering visiting her mother in Ward 241 of Evin Prison.

In the following conversation Hengameh shares her memories and experiences after experiencing solitary confinement four times.

Tell us about the solitary confinement experience.

I was arrested for the first time on 30 July 2009. After my arrest and my admission and after going through the legal process, I was imprisoned in Ward 209 at ten p.m. and beaten and harassed to the point that I was transferred to the ward's medical clinic. The female officers could hardly get me from the basement of the prison to solitary confinement. They didn't pay the slightest attention to my physical condition. I had had heart disease before the arrest and because of the beatings I suffered anxiety attacks. When they took me to the ward's medical clinic, they kept me in bed for about four or five hours. I was in an awful physical condition.

Did you expect such an attitude from the agents of the Ministry of Intelligence?

The agents asked me to confess that I had cooperated with MI6. Since I had studied in the UK, they said that I had worked with MI6 at the time and that I had a connection. They asked me to confess to having illicit affairs with Mr

Khatami[1] and Mr Karroubi,[2] which was unbelievable to me.

I was transferred from the medical clinic to the cell. The person in charge of Ward 209 came to see me. I explained the story to him. He asked me to not respond affirmatively to the interrogators' demands. I felt that he had a different and perhaps a reformist tendency. Maybe it was what he said that gave me the courage to stand up to them during subsequent interrogations and beatings, and not to confess to lies, but only to attending rallies and conducting interviews with news websites as Mr Karroubi's election advisor which, of course, was not a crime.

How were the conditions in the cell?

The cell was 1.2 metres by 2 metres and had a metal washbasin and a toilet. I lived there for seventy-five days. Then I was transferred to a larger cell. There was a basin inside, and we had to go out of the cell to bathe or use the toilet.

1 Sayyid Mohammad Khatami was the fifth president of Iran from 3 August 1997 to 3 August 2005.
2 Mehdi Karroubi is an Iranian Shia cleric leading the National Trust Party. He has been under house arrest since 2011. He has never been tried.

How did it work when you were in this larger cell? How often were you allowed to bathe?

We asked to go to the toilet by pressing a button inside the cell. Every other day we could take a bath and were taken out for fresh air for fifteen minutes.

What were the interrogations like?

I first experienced solitary confinement in 2009. All detainees during this period experienced harsh interrogation conditions. I was no exception. I was divorced and unfortunately I was exposed to sexual charges because of this. Apart from these two people – Mr Karroubi and Mr Khatami – they wanted to connect me to other people from whom they could not get a confession. They pressured me to confess to having sex with people who had not confessed in interrogation. This made my situation exceptionally difficult. Out of my humanist principles, I decided to withstand this line of interrogation and avoid exposing others to a more difficult situation.

When and where did they interrogate you?

My first interrogation was immediately after my admission. It was carried out in the basement of Ward 209 but later I was transferred to Ward 241. I was interrogated in small cells during both the days and nights. One night when I was asleep, maybe at about three in the morning, a female prison guard woke me up. I'd expected this. Because I was constantly threatened with execution, I really thought they were going to execute me, but they were only staging it. I was taken to a room with a rope and told that I would be executed if I did not confess to spying for MI6 and having an illicit affair with Khatami and Karroubi. I fainted out of fear. When I woke up, the morning call to prayer was over. I vented my rage and fear by cursing them. I didn't know where I was. It was an unfamiliar place to me, and I was only taken there once.

How did the interrogators behave during the interrogations?

Unfortunately, the interrogations of 2009 were carried out by young and inexperienced people and those who had recently entered the Ministry, eager to be promoted. These young interrogators were deployed not only for me but also for older and more experienced people. I called the interrogator an intern. He had no will of his own. I identified the head of my interrogation team after my release because I had seen him standing in the doorway from under the blindfold once after forty days of having no news of my family, when I was taken to a room to make a phone call. I remembered his voice from the first day; he spoke in the Isfahani dialect. He sometimes came to the interrogations, but my interrogation was done mainly by the young 'intern'. I was interrogated by him and the Ministry of Intelligence's counter-intelligence team for about twenty-five days. The interrogations lasted from five in the morning until about ten at night. The behaviour of the main interrogator, Amir Hossein Asgari, known as Mahdavi, was terrible and he used obscenities and vulgar words, but the 'intern' tried to play the role of the good guy and brought their questions to me for answers.

After a while, a person called 'Doctor' would also join the interrogations. He tried to act as if he had fallen in love with me. Once, he summoned me to an interrogation room in Ward 241 when there was nothing to be interrogated for and he interrogated my cellmate, Ms F, in the next cell. He sexually harassed her multiple times – asking her how much her breasts cost and putting 5,000 toman notes on them. We agreed that if 'Doctor' bothered her in this way, she would feign nausea so that he would call me from the next cell to help her, as I was a woman and the others were men. One day 'Doctor' came to my cell and showed me a piece of paper with 'I love you' written on it. He put his hand on my head, unexpectedly. I told him that he was not a *mahram* to me and he had no right to touch my head. Obviously, he justified this by saying that my chador and blindfold worked as a boundary between my head and his hands, so there was no problem. When I was released, he watched me from inside his car in front of Evin Prison. He proposed to me and promised that if I married him, he would close my case forever.

Did this 'Doctor' contact you again after your release?

He called me once and made an appointment to return the files in a suitcase to me. He asked me that day if I had changed my mind about marriage. I said I was willing to accept any sentence imposed on me but wouldn't want to see him ever again.

After being detained in solitary confinement for four and a half months in 2009 and then released on bail, you were arrested for a second time. What happened? Where were you taken?

On 27 March 2010, after security officials phoned me, I went to the building of the Ministry of Intelligence. They said they would have a short Q & A, but I was arrested without any such Q & A. This time, the arrest was because, through a former staff member of the Ministry of Intelligence who was fired in 2008, I had been able to identify the name of the head of the Evin interrogations, and I published his name on the Jaras news website along with a photo of him. The day before the summons and arrest, my sentence had been issued in the Court of Appeals. After issuing the sentence it is not legal to keep the accused in solitary confinement and they should be sent to the general ward. Even though the final verdict had been issued, I was transferred to the security ward and held in solitary confinement for two months. I was notified of the sentence, but I was kept in solitary confinement for two months anyway.

Were you interrogated by the same person?

No, this time I had another interrogator. He threatened me that this time it was different and that he'd keep me in my cell until my hair turned as white as my teeth. His problem with me was that I had revealed details of all my previous interrogations, including interrogators' names.

Who was Amir Hossein Askari, also known as Mahdavi?

He became Jalili's[3] advisor on the nuclear negotiating team and stood behind him in the photos.

What was solitary confinement like this time?

This time my cellmate was with one of the defendants in the Radio Farda[4] case. We were together for a week. Then she was released, and I was left alone. At first my cell was small.

3 Saeed Jalili was secretary of Iran's Supreme National Security Council from 2007 to 2013, and was Iran's nuclear negotiator.

4 Radio Farda is the Iranian branch of Radio Free Europe/Radio Liberty. The Iranian government regards it as a hostile media operation, and one of its journalists, Parnaz Azima, was prohibited from leaving Iran for eight months in 2007.

After three weeks I was taken to a larger cell. I was there for the rest of the month.

Did you go on hunger strike during these two arrests?

During my first detention I went on a hunger strike when I lost hope of freedom. I went on strike for eight days. I was taken to the Revolutionary Court and to Judge Pir Abbasi. I was very weak and felt semi-conscious. I was so sick that they brought medical help. Seeing my physical condition, he promised to release me on bail and asked me to end the strike. I told him I'd do so only if they upheld habeas corpus. I ended my strike when they did so and was released the same night.

Tell us about your third experience, and how you were arrested and why.

I was arrested for the third time on 10 March 2017 in Mashhad. I was at my grandmother's funeral. When I was arrested, I was in the detention centre of the Ministry of Intelligence for one night. In the morning I was transferred to the prosecutor's office, and after being arraigned I was transferred to Tehran on a security flight and brought to Ward 209 of Evin Prison. Since Nowruz was approaching, I was taken to the second branch of culture and media with investigator Bizhan Ghasemzadeh immediately the next day. After reading the allegations of being linked to Amadnews,[5] I was again transferred to solitary confinement in Ward 209, immediately after which interrogations began.

How did the interrogators behave this time?

My interrogator was so unpleasant that there were several clashes between him and me. We were in fierce conflict. During one of the interrogations, when he was leaving the room, he told me sarcastically that I deserved to be in Ghezel Hesar[6] Prison. I, of course, replied that considering the way he treated the prisoners, his place was Tehran's Zoo. After these clashes, the Ministry of Intelligence realized that it was not possible to continue the interrogation in this way and changed their methods.

After this interrogator, another one came whom they also called 'Doctor' and he behaved politely. I think that during the interrogation he realized I was innocent, because there was really no evidence for my conviction. After interrogations, on 10 April 2017, I was transferred from Ward 209 of the Ministry of Intelligence to Ward 241 by order of the prosecutor and his deputy, Amir Ghotbi, who was also the head of the Culture and Media Court.

5 Amadnews is a Telegram channel formerly run by Ruhollah Zam. Zam was kidnapped in Iraq, taken to Iran and forced to confess under torture and executed without even being told about the conviction, on 12 December 2020.
6 Ghezel Hesar Prison, in Karaj, is Iran's largest (holding 20,000), and infamous for its appalling conditions.

Tell us about the conditions of solitary confinement in Ward 241.

The cell in Ward 241 was different from 209. The bathroom and toilet were behind a half wall inside the cell. The cell was about 2.5 metres by 2.5 metres. A 360-degree CCTV camera monitored all our cell life. We had to use the washbasin and toilet and bathe in front of the camera and the officers. This was one of the examples of psychological torture for me.

Did you go on a hunger strike during this period as well?

From the moment of my arrest, I had told my family that I would go on a hunger strike. I did not eat for the first 110 days. One of the judiciary's information security interrogators, who had studied paramedic science, supervised my regular tests.

My kidneys were seriously damaged. They were infected and the infection had entered my bloodstream. They had to give me strong antibiotics. For six months, there were several days where I didn't drink any water and this made my condition dangerous. I fainted once and was taken to 241 Medical Centre. When I came to, I was given a serum injection. The situation was tough for me.

Why did you insist on continuing the hunger strike?

I wanted to resist and protest the oppression and injustice imposed on me. If there was one single document to prove that I'd been guilty, I would have had no objection, but I was kept in solitary confinement for six months without any proof. The hunger strike was my expression of rage at the oppression to which I was subjected. This reaction bolstered me mentally. I feel that the pressure I am putting on the judiciary by going on hunger strike is a kind of revenge. When I shifted to a dry hunger strike from a wet hunger strike, I really saw death with my own eyes, but I felt acquiescent about dying on a hunger strike. I felt relieved thinking that I would enact vengeance on those who had cruelly imprisoned me.

Did you have the opportunity to read or do anything to pass the time in the cell?

All I had were books. I was denied the right to communicate with others and to be informed of the news and current affairs through newspapers and television, as well as pen and paper.

Did they allow you to meet your family or make phone calls?

I had a face-to-face meeting with my family once every two weeks, and in between I had a phone call once a week.

What were you given to wear?

In 2009 we wore the usual prison uniforms. It was the same in 2016. In Ward 209 the clothes were white with grey stripes. In Ward 241 the clothes were light blue with horizontal dark stripes. In fact, the clothes were for men in both sections, but they gave them to women prisoners too.

What were the hygiene conditions in Ward 241 like?

Compared to Ward 241, I would say that hygiene in 209 was much better, because the bathroom was outside the cell. In 241 the bathroom and toilet were inside the cell, so the humidity of the environment was annoying. It could also cause diseases. There was no ventilation and the humidity and stench were irritating. Once a week they gave us cleaning material; it wasn't sufficient.

Did you get fresh air?

We had twenty minutes a day.

Where did you go for this?

In Ward 209 there was a space under a pitched roof, about twenty steps by twenty steps. There were no plants there. The courtyard and the walls were concrete and lifeless, but I can say the courtyard of Ward 241 was the only beautiful thing there was in the prison. It seemed to have been a garden with fruit trees previously. Of course, it was separated from the prisoners' walking space by iron fencing, but it could still be seen. There was sports equipment in the yard like the kind usually found in parks, and their colours buoyed the prisoners' moods.

Did you experience solitary confinement again?

Yes, I was arrested on 2 July 2016 in Kish. I had just come out of the cardiac care unit. After my arrest I was transferred to Tehran on a security flight and handed over to Ward 241. During the eleven months of detention, I was alone in solitary confinement with no television or radio. I was not interrogated once during this period.

Did your previous experience help you?

I was admitted to where I had been six months before and experienced the same cells again. I was transferred to the same 2.5 by 2.5-metre cell that had a bathroom and toilet inside. I was kept under that white light for twenty-four hours, which was a kind of torture.

Can you tell us about your feelings during the long solitary months, and the difference between the first months and the last months?

I was banned from calls and visits for seven months. After seven months I was allowed telephone calls and visits once every two weeks, with the permission of Judge Salavati. I felt unhinged in the first months as my personal and social connections were cut off and I had no news of my family. When the investigator repealed my 200 million tomans bail ($47,493) and ordered my temporary detention, I went on a hunger strike that lasted for thirty days. Being deprived of the right to make phone calls and meet my family was another reason for going on a strike. I was furious.

The plaintiff in my case was the head of the judiciary, Sadegh Larijani, and I shouted 'Death to Larijani' several times out of anger in 241. I had nothing to do to pass the time. They didn't give me a television, but they did give me books. I spent all my time reading. If the books ran out, the ward manager (Ali Maleki) would provide me with books from other prisons' libraries. I was very anxious when I did not have books, but when I had something to read, my situation was different. I read an average of about eight hundred pages a day, and it greatly helped in getting through the day.

I would get up at seven in the morning to eat breakfast, and at nine in the evening I would have dinner and then go to bed in the middle of the night. Given that I had endured a severe mental condition, I certainly could not sleep without sleeping pills. Without them, I slept no more than two hours in twenty-four. I also suffer from fibromyalgia. As the disease worsened, I had to take sedatives to obtain a minimum level of tranquillity in solitary confinement. I'd never needed to take them before.

Did you have access to a doctor and medicine for treatment of your heart disease?

Because of this condition, I constantly needed a doctor or a specialist in various fields. The security officers coordinated visits from the doctors, and the necessary medicines were provided.

How much did the prolonged solitary confinement affect your mental and physical condition?

In the first days and months of detention I had not yet oriented myself because I hadn't been interrogated and I was left in the cell. I wanted to be interrogated so that I could talk to someone. Of course, with the permission of the warden, the officers talked to me for about fifteen minutes during the day so that I would not become mentally disturbed, but after a while I got into the routine of solitary confinement. Based on previous experiences, I exercised for two hours a day between reading hours. I either walked in the cell or did long stretching exercises. Sometimes I walked seven kilometres a day in my cell. I'd calculated it this way: once going around the cell and once returning would be about five metres, and a round of prayer-beads with a hundred pieces would be five hundred metres, and fourteen rounds would be seven kilometres.

I did the fourteen rosary rounds with date kernels. Little by little I got used to solitary confinement and even imprisonment. If one day the prison guard was absent, I would ask about her as if one of the family members was missing. The behaviour of Ward 241 female officers was quite different from that of Ward 209 female officers, even in appearance and manner of dress. They were typically between twenty-three and forty-five years old and well-dressed and fashionable, but Ward 209 officers were forty years old or older and wore formal attire and uniforms. Some of the 241 female officers even walked around the ward in informal clothes, which was very good for my mood.

What colour was the cell?

All the cell walls were cream-coloured. Ward 241 is one of the good buildings of Evin. In 241, blindfolds were not usually used, but in 209 blindfolds were required even to go to the bathroom or to be taken out for fresh air, but in 241 these regulations did not exist. As a result, our eyes did not suffer strain. When I compared the 241 cells and the space of the ward with 209, I saw how old the space of 209 was. Overall, Ward 209 is grey compared to 241. I was in 241 twice and the manager met me twice during that time.

How important was meeting your family?
What effect did it have on you?

It was vital to me. I visited my family after seven months. Before my arrest, I had vacated my house and handed it over to the landlord. I went from city to city because I knew that they were going to arrest me. I was deprived of being with my family for about a year. I didn't even have a phone number. I could only call them through the apps of the people who were their guests. Truly, nothing could compare to a face-to-face meeting. When they eventually said I was meeting with my family, after seven months, I couldn't believe that the judge had lifted the ban on phone calls and visits. I thought that they were deceiving me and wanted to hand me over to the IRGC. I calmed down after meeting my family.

How would you summarize your
experience of solitary confinement?

Solitary confinement is a place of torture. It is a grave torture, regardless of the circumstances of the prisoner. Now, if they make the situation even harder, the torture is doubled. As an example, in 2009, in addition to solitary confinement there were beatings, obscenities and hunger strikes. There were other hardships in later prison sentences, on top of what had already existed, and that's why I went on a hunger strike. Prohibition of contact and visits made it even harder to tolerate the situation in the cell. The light that was on at all times day and night irritated my eyes, deprived me of sleep and was a kind of torture. I endured difficult situations when I was confronted with vulgar words and sexual insults. I was completely disturbed when I heard the cries and lamentations of ISIS men in the nearby cells who were to be executed. In one of the wards behind the cell, I heard the cries of women who had been harassed. These voices are my worst memories of solitary confinement.

REYHANEH TABATABAI

Reyhaneh Tabatabai is a journalist, political activist and supporter of the Islamic Iran Participation Front.[1]

She spent a year in the women's ward of Evin Prison from 12 January 2016. In addition to being sentenced to one year she was banned from membership in political parties and groups, as well as banned from media and virtual networks for two years. Her case was opened by the IRGC, and she was charged with membership in the National Youth Headquarters in the 2014 elections, participating in a reformist youth conference in Shahrekord, and insulting Saeed Jalili and Mohammad Baqer Qalibaf[2] on Facebook.

Reyhaneh had previously been arrested three times and imprisoned in the women's ward of Evin Prison. The first time was on 13 December 2010, and the second in the winter of 2014, during the widespread detention of Iranian

---

1 A government-oriented reformist political party in Iran.
2 Mohammad Bagher Ghalibaf was the mayor of Tehran from 2005 to 2017.

journalists, which eventually led to the court ruling 'ban on prosecution'. She was arrested for the third time on 20 June 2014, when she was detained for six months on charges of propaganda against the regime, which was related to her arrest in 2010 by the IRGC.

The size of the cell was about the size of a normal room and you could walk in it. It had two windows attached to the ceiling, but it was not possible to see the sky through them. The light inside the cell consisted of three lights, one lit by day and three by night. The toilet was inside, separated from the cell by a door.

There was no radiator, and the heater was a vent through which hot air came in, but because it had an annoying sound, I wanted it to be turned off. There were four or five military blankets in the room, the floor was carpeted and, of course, clean. The door would not open unless the prisoner called the guards to ask for something, or when they brought food in the morning, at noon and at night. Tea was served in the morning and evening. I was taken out for fresh air every morning and evening for twenty minutes, and I was the only prisoner in that ward at the time. The ward lay in absolute silence and isolation. I thought that if something happened to me inside the cell they wouldn't notice, given the distance of the guard's room from me. So, I was very worried about what would happen.

In terms of clothing, our uniform consisted of a pink coat and a pair of trousers. I was given two sets of these clothes to wash and change. The food came from Sarollah Camp[3] and the quality was good. I had fruit every other day. I was interrogated every day and I became so tired that when I came back, I fell asleep immediately. The interrogation started at around noon and continued until sunset. I was usually fasting, so I was interrogated until iftar. I was even interrogated on the days of Tasua, Ashura and Fridays. Sometimes the interrogations lasted up to eleven or twelve at night, and once it even went on until two or three in the morning.

The first day I entered the detention centre I was sleepy because I had been awake until seven in the morning. Arrest and admission formalities were carried out, and I went into the cell and slept. When I entered the cell, I saw some dead beetles on the floor. They had just sprayed pesticides. They took my clothes and gave me prison clothes. After a short while they called me for interrogation. I was blindfolded and had to put on a chador for going there. I walked across the yard to the interrogation room and sat on a chair with my eyes to the wall.

I filled out a form. The interrogator said that as far as he knew the accused, he expected that she would behave like this. I wanted to laugh. He wanted to say that he knew about

3 Sarollah Camp was established in 1995, and is at the core of the IRGC's attempts to control Tehran. It is supervised by the IRGC's commander in chief, and has close links with the Ministry of Intelligence.

my personality. He, indeed, told me all the information he had about me, including the coffee shops I had visited and parts of my conversations in different places. He even mentioned 'intimate' family matters. He gave detailed information about various family events to claim that he knew everything about me.

They took my email address and password and said I would be there for six or seven months, unless I took a pen and paper and wrote everything myself and cooperated.

There was a Qur'an in my cell. There was a dead beetle in the corner, so I asked for it to be cleaned. They did. The next day the second team interrogated me. The interrogator on the first team had asked me not to tell the second team that I was fine, because they would become angry. It was only after two days of interrogations that I was charged. I was handcuffed when taken to the prosecutor's office to be arraigned, to which the investigator objected. I couldn't have phone calls for the first two weeks. After that, I was given a phone to call my family three times in thirty-six days, but I didn't get to see them.

The interrogations took place in one section of Ward 2A. The interrogator never came into this room, instead questioning me from behind a screen. I could smoke in the interrogation room, but smoking inside the cell and in the yard was forbidden.

Because of my activities during 2009, I was already sure that I would be arrested, so I was prepared. I had a lot of sympathy with the Green Movement. A year before I was arrested, I had heard many stories about solitary confinement, and now I tried to use the experiences of others to strengthen myself and my resilience, so that I could keep my spirits high.

My next interrogations were about my activities. I was asked to speak out against Fakhrossadat Mohtashamipour[4] and Mr Tajzadeh,[5] and at the same time they asked me questions about my relationship with foreigners and journalists abroad.

At first, because they had access to my laptop, they asked a lot of questions beyond the remit of the charges, but I did not open up about these issues. They even asked about non-political issues and my family and friends, but due to my disciplined attitude they couldn't delve into these matters in any depth.

On Ashura, after they claimed that I had not answered some questions accurately or that I had lied, they started to shout and threaten me. This made me take responsibility for my actions, but I didn't confess anything that would implicate other people.

Thereafter, I accepted responsibility for all my actions and proudly wrote on all the interrogation sheets that I worked for the *Kaleme* website because people had the right to know

4 Fakhrossadat Mohtashamipour is the head of the women's section of the Islamic Iran Participation Front.
5 Sayyid Mostafa Tajzadeh was held in Evin Prison from 2009 until 2016. A reformist, he belongs to the Islamic Iran Participation Front.

what was going on in the country.[6] I wrote that I supported
the Green Movement and its prisoners. I was finally released
on 100 million tomans ($23,612) bail after thirty-six days in
solitary confinement.

Second arrest, 3 February 2013

*Ward 209 of the Ministry of Intelligence Security Detention
Centre*

I had left the newspaper building for an interview. My friends
called and told me not to go to back because they had come to
arrest me and a few other colleagues. I stayed out until ten
o'clock at night, but eventually I decided to go home and
thought that if they wanted, they would arrest me immediately. At home I learned that fourteen or fifteen other journalists had been arrested that day. After a few days, at ten o'clock
in the morning on the twelfth of Bahman, my father came in
and said that two cars were parked in front of the door. I called
them from the window and invited them into the house. They
first tried to say that they were anti-narcotics police and they
had come to arrest a neighbour. I told them not to kid around
and said that we lived on the first floor. They entered and I
was arrested after a house search.

I was admitted to Ward 209 and taken to a cell. Upon
arrival I saw that the cell was very dirty. It had a small

6 *Kaleme* is an Iranian online news outlet, closely affiliated with the reformist
Green Movement.

washbasin, but no toilet. It was a men's ward, and I could hear their voices. I think I went to interrogation the next day, and three days later I was arraigned.

I was taken to another cell two days later. In my situation, I hadn't expected to be arrested at all. A few days before my arrest, I went to the IRGC follow-up office and was interrogated for about five hours. So, there was no reason to detain me. However, the Ministry of Intelligence had published a statement before I was arrested implying that several other people might be arrested.

I was questioned in interrogation cells in the public corridor, on the same floor as my cell. I had to walk blindfolded to and from these interrogations, and was made to face the wall while I was being questioned. The interrogator would say he would come the next day, but then he wouldn't come for five or six days, and the worst thing was that I had to wait alone and silent inside the cell. This method was completely different from the IRGC's, as they would return at the appointed time for interrogation. I had longer hours of interrogation in Ward 2A. So, I wasn't in the cell as often. Since it was the first time, I read the Qur'an and *Mafatih al-Jinan*, which was useful and exciting for me. The interrogators advised me to pray in order to pass time in the cell. They said they knew how hard it was to endure such an environment when the door closed on the prisoner. In 209, in addition to having few interrogations, I waited for many hours. I was interrogated three times a month, four or five hours each time.

In 209 there was no toilet inside the cell, and I had trouble going to the toilet. I could not turn on the lights at night and go to the bathroom. The guards' snarling made me nervous and uncomfortable. I fasted most of the days and did not eat lunch, except for a few days. The evenings were also very bad and I couldn't eat. They gave me fruit once a week, which I rationed and ate throughout the week.

In 209 I felt dejected and cried. I missed my mother. The feeling of nostalgia and the desire to escape and get out of that cell put a lot of pressure on me. Because I had no TV or radio, it was very difficult to fill my day. Sometimes I felt depressed. A few days after my arrest, I was once given the *Bahar*[7] newspaper. I read news of my arrest and that of other journalists and I was extremely excited. Except that one time the only newspaper they gave me was *Ettela'at*.[8]

In the cell I was given the book *Da*[9] which is about seven hundred pages long, and I read it seven times. After I read the first hundred pages, I went back to the beginning so that the book would not end soon. After *Da*, I asked for other novels, but they wouldn't give them to me. Later I realized how reading this book and imagining scenes of war and killing and death in a cell put more strain on me and crushed my spirit.

7 *Bahar* (The Spring) is an Iranian reformist newspaper.

8 *Ettela'at* is the oldest Persian paper in Iran, now used as a propaganda instrument by the regime.

9 *Da* (Mother) is a memoir by Seyyedeh Zahra Hosseini detailing her experiences during the Iran–Iraq War.

In section 209, unlike 2A, I could call my family once or twice a week. I was sleepless at night but didn't want to go to the hospital. A few days before the end of my detention I had severe palpitations, but they said the doctor wasn't present at the medical centre and waited until night to take me to a hospital.

The behaviour of the guards in 2A was better than 209. In 209, the guards were rude and apparently trained to harass prisoners, to be indifferent to their requests and to ignore their problems. I wasn't allowed to meet my family during the time I was in 209. There were now seventeen of us who were arrested together, and some were transferred to General Ward 209 two weeks later, but I was in the cell until the last day. I was supposed to be taken to a general ward in the last days, but they said it wasn't possible because they didn't have a suitable cellmate to share with me. They didn't even give me a television and said, 'you'd commit suicide if we gave you a TV'. They said they couldn't release me soon because they were stuck on my case while foreign circles and media were protesting about my detention.

I think the reason was that they had no evidence against us. They talked about the BBC and other foreign media all the time.

Inside the cells we wore a blouse and trousers, but we had to wear a chador and a headscarf when we were taken to interrogation. They didn't take our bras in 2A, but in 209 we were not allowed to wear a bra from the beginning. The writings on the walls in 2A made it look haunted. They were mostly written by people with serious allegations. But the ones in 209 were written by people I was familiar with. Some were written with a pen; others were scratched into the wall. On the wall of the toilet in 2A was a painting of a house where a person lived with her parents. This painting gave me a strange feeling. I enjoyed looking at it.

The fresh air hour in 209 was not truly a fresh air hour because we were taken to a patio, above which was a glass roof. In the cell I walked a lot and exercised; I lay down and sat down. I filled my time with making things – for instance I made prayer beads with orange peel or found something to measure time with. I was able to sleep only when they gave me a chador for prayer because the military blankets were too rough.

SIMA KIANI

Sima Kiani is a Bahá'í, was born in 1965, and has lived in Shahr-e Rey since 1970.

She was first arrested by the security forces on 9 March 2017 and was released on a bail of 200 million tomans ($47,225) in April 2017.

She was a member of a group of servants of the Faith that administered Bahá'í affairs. She was sentenced by the Revolutionary Court of Rey to one year in prison on charges of 'propaganda against the regime'.

'The intelligence service was always aware of our activities, especially since 1997 when they raided our house and arrested and interrogated my father, who was also a member of the servants at that time. I was also a member and from time to time I would call another of the servants and talk to them about our community, which became one of the serious allegations against me after my arrest,' Sima explains.

I woke up on 9 March 2017 at 7.30 in the morning, with the security agents ringing the doorbell. Seven officers entered the house after showing their search warrant and immediately began searching our house. My elderly parents were also at home and were shocked by the sudden entrance of the officers.

They searched our home and threatened us. My mother was repeatedly told that if I cooperated, I would return home very soon, in two or three hours.

After inspecting the house, I was transferred to the Shahr-e-Rey follow-up office, and after initial interrogations and numerous threats I was transferred to the prosecutor's office and from there to Evin.

I'd thought I was going to be taken to a public ward. I had no conception of imprisonment or solitary confinement. After arriving in Evin and taking care of the initial formalities, they allowed me to contact my family. To my surprise they took me to a three-by-two-metre room and gave me special clothes. I realized that I was going to be alone, but I didn't know where in Evin I was.

After two days the interrogators came to see me and, according to them, they had left me alone for two days to think about and understand where I was. Interrogations began. I was interrogated for ten days in a row. The interrogations were done politely but were tense. They threatened to arrest other family members and transfer me from there to another prison and not allow me to see my family again.

During my solitary confinement, I called my family two or three times. My family had come to Evin many times and each time they were told that I wasn't here.

I was interrogated for ten days in a room which they said was not an interrogation room but a place for conversation. It was a furnished and relatively large room. The interrogations were carried out face to face, without a blindfold. They said we were just having a talk.

Those were ten days of threats and intimidation. Every day, at the end of the interrogation, they would ask questions about people around me, my activities or my past, and they would give me a number of interrogation papers so that I could write the answers to the questions in my cell at night. In the mornings they checked what I had written and always said that it wasn't what they wanted. Then they'd go on yelling at me and threatening me, saying that I wouldn't be released after the interrogations and that I'd either be transferred to another prison or left where I was to rot away.

During the interrogation and my time in solitary confinement, what bothered me the most was that there was nothing to entertainment myself with, no books, no newspapers, nothing. It was exceptionally difficult for me to spend my days like that. I spent part of my time in prayer and supplication. I tried to sleep so that I might lose track of time. My cell was close to the prison guards' office, and I would always hear the incomprehensible sound of television programmes. To pass the time I tried to recognize the unintelligible words and I made progress, so that over the days the sounds became more discernible to me.

The ten days of interrogations were better days because my day was full. In general, I was so lonely and bored with having nothing to do in solitary confinement that I preferred to be interrogated rather than left alone in a cell. I was blindfolded and accompanied by a female guard from the IRGC, and then taken to another place about fifteen minutes away. They did not even allow the female guard to be there. In that building, from the sounds I heard, it seemed only the men moved around. They put me against the wall without any explanations. About half an hour later, someone, who may have seen that I was worried, said, 'Your interrogators are late, but they are on their way.'

After about an hour, men from the Ministry of Intelligence arrived and took me to a quite small room. One of the interrogators was also there. They told me to write that I regretted my actions and that I promised to cooperate with the Ministry of Intelligence. When confronted with my refusal, they began to threaten me aggressively; they said that my friends and family would be arrested. They told me again to cooperate, and when I declined, they said that the situation would change from then on. 'You haven't had a real interrogation!' they said. 'You asked for it. As of tomorrow, you will be interrogated with your eyes to the wall.' That was what they did. I think they took me to another place to intimidate me.

In short, after all the threats they returned me to my cell. From the next day, interrogations continued facing the wall until we reached Nowruz holidays. Before Nowruz, on 20 March, the interrogations were almost over and they took the necessary signatures to confirm what they called 'confessions'.

The beginning of the holidays was the worst time in solitary confinement. The days would hardly pass and there was nothing to do. They were the rainy days of April. The sole way of glimpsing the outside world was through a small hatch up against the ceiling and covered with lace. Three or four times a day the jailer would open the door for food, tea, or medicine. I waited impatiently. I could tell the time by these little things; breakfast was from 7.30 to 8, lunch from 12 to 12.30 and dinner around 7. I pricked up my ears to hear the surroundings, and I entertained myself.

I was completely insomniac and slept for maybe an hour or two during the day and I lost all appetite, but I also had some very enjoyable times, increasing in length and quality over time. I had never felt as close to Bahá'u'lláh and God as I did in those days. I felt like I was in a monastery, and this was an opportunity that life had given me to think and pray and to be alone with myself and Bahá'u'lláh.

It was an incredible feeling to have to make the most of these very difficult days, which I had never experienced before. I felt that whatever I wanted would be fulfilled, but I wanted nothing except the satisfaction of Bahá'u'lláh. It was a peculiar feeling. I felt that Bahá'u'lláh had taken me out of my daily life and provided me with an exceptional opportunity to be alone with Him. These moments were inexpressibly magnificent. It made me feel so strong that I thought I could handle anything.

I did not have any interrogations during the thirteen days of Nowruz holidays. The only different moments I looked forward to were the fresh air time, every other day for twenty minutes. Gradually, as the guards became acquainted with me, they allowed me to be out for half an hour or more. It was one of the most enjoyable times of solitary confinement because I could walk in the courtyard with its transparent roof, in mostly rainy weather, praying aloud and shedding tears.

I felt very light when I went back to my cell.

As time went on, I became more insomniac. I was almost sleepless and would just doze off for a few minutes every few hours. I scarcely ate and had kidney problems and dehydration as well. So, on 4 April due to anxiety and dehydration, my blood pressure ran so high that I was taken to the ward's medical centre.

On 4 April at nine a.m. they told me to get ready. 'Go downstairs,' they said. 'The interrogators have come to see you.' When I went to the room, the interrogators were shocked to see my face. The first sentence of one of them said was, 'Twenty-seven days of solitary confinement has worked.' 'Why are you keeping me here?' I asked them. 'I'm sick. My parents need me.' They replied that I would only be allowed to leave the prison when the interrogations finished.

When they saw my desire to be released, they said that being released was not that easy and I had to be filmed confessing to what I'd done. They said that even after being released, the interrogations would continue. And that was what they did. That is, after my release, I was summoned to the city follow-up office for several sessions and interrogated and threatened until they reached a dead end with me, as they put it, and stopped interrogating me.

I strongly opposed filming. They said that was the only way. I had lost about seven kilos and was dehydrated. As a result of the discomfort, my left kidney was severely painful and my left eye almost blind. After my release the doctor told me that I suffered from severe corneal swelling due to anxiety.

The next day they started to pressure and threaten me even more. 'You will be kept here until you are forgotten,' they said. 'Or we will transfer you to prison in complete isolation until the trial.' In brief, the tensions continued as before. They emphasized that the only condition for my release was to be filmed. Otherwise, they said I'd not be taken to court for trial. 'In the film,' they explained, 'you'll talk only about the things you've already confessed to.' I asked for a chance to think. I went back to my cell and prayed for hours and then accepted their offer.

Based on what they'd explained to me, the filming scenario was such that they said it would be filmed in three episodes or parts. 'In the first episode you'll introduce yourself,' they explained. 'In the second one, you'll talk about your propaganda activity, and in the third part, you'll talk about the

Bahá'í Yaran, and your communications during their admin-istration of the Bahá'í community. You'll also explain how the Bahá'í Yaran committee registered Bahá'u'lláh's house as a cultural heritage site.' They said I had to give them any information I had about these points. They instructed me not to look at the interrogator who was present when I was being filmed. They wanted to take away the chador I usually wore during interrogations, which I strongly opposed. During the filming I was the only speaker and I spoke descriptively. There were no questions and answers. After the filming, bail was issued, and I was released two days later.

An hour before my release I was transferred from my cell to another where a female journalist was imprisoned. It was only in the last hours of my imprisonment that I realized I was in security Ward 209 of Evin Prison.

Finally, on the afternoon of 7 April, I left this ward. It was a unique, perhaps once-in-a-lifetime experience, agonizing but exceptionally spiritual. I hope its good effects will last for the rest of my life.

I know that the future of my country is bright, and in the future, prejudice, hatred and enmity will vanish from this land.

FATEMEH MOHAMMADI

Fatemeh Mohammadi (born in 1998) is a civil activist and was arrested by the Ministry of Intelligence for converting to Christianity and attending religious services in private homes. She was arrested during a ceremony at the house of a Christian in Tehran. On 7 April 2016, in Branch 26 of the Revolutionary Court of Tehran presided over by Judge Ahmadzadeh, she was sentenced to six months in prison on the charges of 'Christian activity and acting against national security through propaganda against the state' and transferred to the security Ward 209 of Evin Prison. Fatemeh spent twenty days in solitary confinement in this ward. She was banned from studying English translation at Azad University, Tehran Campus, due to her conversion to Christianity.

What were the conditions of the cells
in which you were imprisoned?

I was imprisoned in two cells at different times for thirty-nine days. Both cells had cream-coloured walls and ceilings. A piece of ragged brown carpet covered the floor of the cell. I was in a very small cell for the first three days. It was so small that you couldn't walk in it. There was something like a window high up, just below the ceiling. A perforated plate was installed behind the window. I could not see the sky at all from behind this. I could only tell whether it was day or night. After three days I was transferred to a cell that was twice the size of the previous cell. It was the same shape as the first cell, there were toilets in both cells, but the toilet in the small cell was very unhygienic.

I had a towel, a toothbrush and toothpaste, which they would take from me after I used them. I was not allowed to bring them with me into the cell. For interrogation I had to wear a coat, headscarf and chador, all of which were taken back at the end. I entered the cell with nothing. There was nothing inside the cell either, not a notebook or a pen or anything you could use to entertain yourself with. The cell was very dark and my eyes were very irritated in the weak light. It was hard for me to endure.

How often were you allowed to shower?

I was allowed to take a shower three times a week for about twenty minutes and a maximum of thirty minutes. When it took a few more minutes the officers started yelling at me. 'What are you doing?' they shouted. 'Get out!' On the door to the bathroom was a small hatch that they frequently opened to see through into the bathroom. I became terribly upset and protested, but they stood there, yelling at me to come out. To go to the toilet, I had to press a button that would turn on my cell light in the officers' room so that they could come and take me to the bathroom. Every time I pressed the button the officers came in bad-tempered, yelling at me about why I went to the toilet so frequently, and their anger and the fights made me more cautious about drinking water. So I drank less water. It was very hard for me as I could ask for nothing without being abused, not even going to the bathroom and toilet. Everything was so nerve-wracking.

When I was in the small cell, the toilet was very old and dirty and the officers said that I had to use it whenever I needed it, but occasionally they would open the door and look into the cell. It made me feel unsafe using that toilet.

Did they take you out for fresh air?

Yes, for twenty to thirty minutes, two times a week. I was in the yard for a maximum of an hour a week. The yard walls were very high and had a camera. Its roof was covered with iron bars and a thin layer of talcum was placed on the bars.

What did you do in the cell and how did you spend your time?

For the first three days when I was in the small cell, I had to do everything inside the cell and I wasn't even allowed to go to the bathroom. It was tough. I am an active person and I had to try to make myself feel different. At night sometimes I would lean my head against the wall of the cell or the toilet bowl which smelled awful and made me sick. There was nothing inside the cell that I could do. I felt that time was standing still.

How were the interrogations?

The interrogations were overwhelming. I cried for hours when I returned to my cell from interrogation. For the first few days I felt so bad that I even forgot to wash my face. I remember that on the third day of detention, when I was taken out of the cell for interrogation, the officers told me that the skin around my eyes was black. I realized that I hadn't washed my face in these three days and my eye make-up had smudged.

I hadn't been allowed to take a bath until that day. Before my arrest, I had depression. When I entered the cell in such a condition, I tried to comfort myself. I gave myself hope. But after a few days, it didn't work any more. Obviously, the interrogators made me feel worse. During interrogations, my family and I, and especially my mother, were openly insulted. They mocked and denigrated my faith to humiliate me. For example, they called the church a casino or they said 'What is this Bible book you are reading? Go read the Qur'an.'

They would delve into the most private corners of my life, which had nothing to do with the accusations against me, and they would say derogatory things. They would interfere in my family's private affairs, judge and insult. My father was called dishonourable, and I was defenceless. I remember crying one day, saying that I loved my father, and the interrogator became silent. Well, the interrogators had taken my mobile phone and brought up all the conversations between me and my friends, which were personal and private and basically had nothing to do with my case and the accusations, and they questioned me about them in the interrogation cell.

Naturally, every human being has private, friendly and emotional relationships with their family, acquaintances and friends, but the interrogators did not respect this in any way. It astounded me. One day the guard of the ward called me out of the cell, sat in front of me and told me to take off my blindfold. Then he started asking questions about my most personal issues. He was just a male guard, but he saw fit to know about my private matters and even ask me about them to insult and humiliate me.

I wondered why I was blindfolded and facing the wall when I was interrogated about Christianity, and they only removed my blindfold when I had to write. Whereas when they wanted to talk to me about my personal issues as a woman, they took off the blindfold and I could see them. I did not have any moral objections to this, but it is a matter of a person's privacy, and no one has the right to violate it and put individuals under psychological pressure, to try to take advantage of them.

Did prison make you ill?

Before my arrest, and at some other points in my life, I suffered from depression. Being detained in solitary confinement and interrogated worsened my condition, due to not having any mobility, while being exposed to absolute silence around the clock.

The interrogators were fully aware of my entire medical record and ongoing treatment and referred to it during the interrogations, but did not allow me to have access to my doctor or medication. Naturally my mental health deteriorated as a result of the stress. I remember one day in my cell I was sick. Out of extreme anxiety, I banged my head against the wall several times. I shouted. Later I was taken for questioning. I cried and said I was not feeling well and needed medicine. After a few hours they took me to the next room where a man told me he was a doctor. I asked him to give me medicine to treat my diagnosed condition that had been aggravated in the cell. He prescribed a pill and told them to give it to me every day.

I never saw the pill cover, but every day and every night they brought me a pill which I took in the presence of the officer with a glass of water. Not only did I not feel better, but I became even more anxious. I noticed this change. I was no longer being interrogated and was left in the cell. This was more annoying and worrying. 'Well, if no one has anything to do with me,' I told the female officers, 'why don't you take me out of the cell?' But they didn't talk to me. I was even willing to leave the cell for interrogation, in which I was always humiliated, insulted and yelled at. I was content with anything that might happen, as long as I could at least hear footsteps and see the world outside the cell. Once, a man came to clean the hallway. All the while that gentleman was sweeping and cleaning the corridor, I held my breath and put my head next to the vent, trying to see him work through a very small hole, but of course I couldn't. Still, I stood behind the door and on my feet all the time.

I didn't know whether I should trust the interrogator or not. I was being interrogated one day. I didn't have a watch but it was late. The interrogator came and said that all my friends and family had given them important information against me and started blaming me. He said, 'Look, even your family is speaking against you.' I believed him. I cried a lot. I asked myself why no one defended me, why everyone had abandoned me. I believed that even my parents were against me and you can't imagine how much my mood declined and how much I cried. I later found out that all this was a lie. Because of the intensity of solitary confinement and interrogation, sometimes I saw myself, crying, fallen on my knees, without being aware of what I was doing. I called out to Christ and talked to him. I felt that no one would reach me except Christ.

SEDIGHEH MORADI

Sedigheh Moradi (born in 1960, Tehran) was arrested twice in the 1980s and has had a difficult time in prison.

After being released from her second arrest Sedigheh got married, and has a daughter named Yasaman. The former political prisoner was arrested again on 1 May 2011 and transferred to Ward 209 of Evin Prison. She was sentenced to ten years in prison by Branch 28 of the Tehran Revolutionary Court on charges of moharebeh and links to anti-regime groups.

Sedigheh was transferred to a public ward after seven months and was released from Evin Prison on 23 December 2016, after serving five years in prison. The Ministry of Intelligence arrested her again in 2019 along with her husband, Mehdi Khawas Sefat.

Tell us about your first experience of being in prison.
I was arrested on 15 June 1981. After my arrest I was transferred to Ishratabad barracks. It was a military detention

centre with solitary confinement. I was there for about five days. Then Mojtaba Halvaei[1] came and put all thirty of us in a van. When the van set off, we all felt awful. The van left Tehran and headed for Karaj. We felt dreadful on the highway. When the car stopped at the gas station, we opened the back of the van so that at least people could see us. Finally, they took us to a barn on the Karaj Road. Two groups of fifteen of us were put in each stall. They locked the stall doors with rods. It was horrible and completely unsanitary. Our only food was bread and cheese. They also gave us large cucumbers at night. Most of us became very weak.

Mr Kachuei[2] came and called us by numbers instead of names. My number was 14. From the next day we were flogged. Most of the prisoners were members of the Mujahedin-e-Khalq organization but three of them were leftists. During the day the stalls were opened for an hour so we could go to the bathroom. We were in the stables for about a month. Then they took us to Ghezel Hesar. We were in Ghezel Hesar from the end of July to February 1981. We had not yet revealed our names to the authorities. When Haj Davood[3] and

1 Mojtaba Halvaei Asgar was the head of security at Evin Prison. He personally tortured prisoners and participated in the prison massacre of 1988.

2 Mohammad Kachuei was the first head of Evin Prison after the Islamic Revolution, who was assassinated on 29 July 1981 by the Mujahedin-e-Khalq Organization.

3 Davood Rahmani, known as Haj Davood, was the first head of Tehran's Ghezel Hesar Prison after the 1957 Iranian Revolution. From the summer of 1981 to July 1984, he was the director of Ghezel Hesar Prison – known as a reign of terror today. He invented many new forms of torture.

Souri[4] came, they discovered our identities. Then we were transferred to Evin. During this time, we were in a public ward. In front of us was a cell for the unmarried prisoners.

There were four hundred of us in four large cells with three beds in each. The way the guards treated the prisoners was strange. For example, Haj Davood would single out anyone who wore a plaid coat or glasses with a black frame. On one occasion, in cell one, there were too many prisoners on the bed so it broke and the prisoners fell on each other's heads and were injured.

Anyway, I was released in March 1981.

Tell us about your experience of solitary confinement when you were arrested for the second time.

I was arrested again in August 1985. They beat and cursed me from the moment I was arrested. It was strange when they asked me my name, surname and shoe size. Then I realized what it was for.

First they took me to a detention centre.

I was alone in the cell. The walls were white and orange. There was nothing in there. There was a window high up on the wall; I had to stretch up to see a small bit of the sky through it. I was in that cell for about two months. I heard the National University bell ring. I was fastened to a bed

4 Hojjatollah Souri was one of the key heads at Ghezel Hesar Prison, and later became the head of Evin Prison. In 2011 he was sanctioned by the European Union for torture and abuse of prisoners.

from the very first time I went for interrogation. They pulled my arms and legs and tied them. It hurt a lot. The cables hit the soles of my feet. My whole body trembled. I cried. It was as if I was dying. The back pain was less severe. They turned my head from behind, which caused damage to my neck. I remember that I fainted and they poured water on me with a pitcher. I could not stand, but they forced me.

Suffering under interrogation and being beaten with cables is more tolerable than hearing the voices of others being flogged. I returned to my cell after having been flogged. I was terribly ill. Downstairs were women's cells and upstairs were the men's cells. When the men upstairs sang, I heard their voices and that gave me strength.

The guards were very frustrating. Every few hours they would open the door and start threatening me. There was a very young girl imprisoned two cells away from mine. I think she was seventeen or eighteen years old. According to the guards, her name was Kajal. She'd endured a lot of torture. Two days later, I heard that she had been taken to be executed. I heard her say that she'd cut the head of an IRGC guard with a sharp tile.

I also heard the voices of elderly mothers. Mothers were asked for their children's addresses. They were questioned about their children's hiding places. They either didn't know or wouldn't say. I remember a sixty-year-old mother who was flogged with cables and returned to the ward because she wouldn't give away where her child was.

How did you fill your time?

I remember one day when I had been flogged with cables and I felt terrible. I sang the songs I could remember. I was single then and didn't live with my family, so I thought about my friends. I occupied my time by thinking about the places I had visited and the things I had done. I didn't have the Qur'an, but I thought about the chapters I had memorized. I recalled movies I had seen.

I had nothing in my cell. At first they wouldn't give me a spoon and when I complained they told me to learn how to eat without one. After a while they gave me an aluminium spoon.

I knew I had to walk, but I couldn't. I lay down most of the time. I spoke out loud and tried to listen to my voice as if it was coming from someone else. There was silence, except when the prisoners sang upstairs. The most beautiful sound was the alarm clock of the National University. I felt like life was going on when, for instance, I heard the sound of a motor-bike, or when I heard the sound of a fruit seller. I felt alive.

What effect did the white colour of the wall and the silence in the cell have on you?

It was devastating. For a long time, it felt as though nothing in the world existed. I don't know how to express it. In those moments it was as if I was far from everything. It was as if I had been forgotten. I prayed for God to help me. I sang everything I knew so that I might not be so anguished by loneliness. One day a butterfly sat on the carpet. I started talking to it. I talked to it as if it were a dear friend. Once the guard came and started cursing me saying we were all crazy. I'd been overjoyed by the presence of the butterfly but didn't say anything about it. Well, I felt distraught at that time because prisoners were being taken for execution. Nonetheless I would reproach myself and say that I was not alone; the prisoners upstairs were my brothers, and the prisoners in the cells alongside mine were my mothers and sisters.

One day the prison guard told me to get ready. I thought I was going to be executed. 'Where are you taking me?' I asked. 'Where you had expected,' he said. I had nothing to take with me. I had a pair of comfortable trousers that I had bought for five hundred tomans. I picked them up and set off. I thought I was going to be executed. How much unfinished work did I have? But time was up. I started reciting the Ayat al-Kursi[5] verse. First, they took me to the warehouse. There were a lot of things there. They gave me my bag and we left. I noticed that there were a lot of people standing in line. I stood behind a girl whose name was Maria. I asked her if she knew where we were going. She didn't know either. Eventually we found out that we were being transferred to the public wards, and as my accusations were political, I was transferred to Ward 209 instead of the public ward.

5 The Throne Verse is the 255th verse of the 2nd Surah of the Quran, Al-Baqarah. It is regarded as a powerful protection in the Islamic world.

Tell us about the 209 cells and your new condition.

The cells were approximately the same size. I entered one –
its door and walls were covered in writing. I read Shamlou's
poems. I read 'Vartan Didn't Say a Word'[6] several times. I
decided not to read them all at once but to read some of them
every day. Inside the cell there was nothing to entertain
myself. I didn't see or hear from anyone. It was tough.
Obviously, I had a plan for myself. I had a plan to read the
Qur'an. I tried not to think about the outside world. One day
I was reading the Qur'an, and when I reached the Surah
Muhammad, the door opened and I was called out. My
mother had come to visit me. I was very happy to finally see
someone, and for my first meeting to be with my mother. She
was in a good mood and she was alone. I was rejuvenated
from seeing her good spirits. She did not have any important
news or information about the organization or my comrades,
but this meeting was good for me.

**How long were you kept in solitary
confinement in 1985?**

I was in solitary confinement in the detention centre for
about a month. Then I was taken to the basement of Ward
209. The cell's ceiling in the detention centre was rotting, and
large beetles fell from it onto my head. It stank of burnt oil.

6 Vartan Salakhanian was a leftist political prisoner who refused to give away
his comrades' names and was tortured to death. Shamlou's poem about him is
popular in Iran.

In 209 the cells were different. My cell was on one of the first floors. I couldn't see the sky. In the detention centre they beat us for information during the interrogations.

When they asked for my shoe size, I said it was 37, but after I was tortured, I had to walk in size 42 slippers. Interrogations at the detention centre were conducted by intelligence agents. There I was kept in solitary confinement for about two months and in Ward 209 for a month. In 209 I was left in the cell without being seriously interrogated. After my interrogation ended in 209, I was sent to Branch Four. I went to a closed room consisting of twenty others from the Tudeh Party[7] and the Aksariat Organization.[8] The interrogation started again in a closed room. When I was in the cell, the sound of the bell and the footsteps of the prison guard passing by my cell made me sick. I breathed a sigh of relief as the jailer passed.

What did you hear from your cellmates?

My fellow prisoners went through hard times in the cell but, for example, Ms Soraya Moradi, a member of Rah-e Kargar,[9] always kept her morale up and gave us courage even though her husband had been executed and she had herself been

7 The Tudeh Party of Iran is an Iranian communist party formed in 1941.

8 The Organization of Iranian People's Fadaian (Majority) is an Iranian left-wing opposition political party in exile, advocating a secular republic.

9 Organization of Revolutionary Workers of Iran is a Marxist–Leninist organization, founded in 1978, currently exiled in Germany.

flogged with cable so much that the skin on the soles of her feet had become as thin as a baby's. I was beaten during interrogations and my eyes were injured, too. To help each other put up with the situation, we summoned up our courage. The food was not bad, but we could not really eat anything.

How would you describe the effects of solitary confinement and torture on your fellow prisoners?

I saw many women whose mental and behavioural balance was disturbed after torture and solitary confinement. A woman named Marzieh talked with herself for hours under the blanket and laughed. She had been severely tortured.

A woman named Nasrin came to us and put her hand out. 'Did you kill my husband?' she said. We'd say no, and she would leave. She ran and repeated her husband's name. I know she had been in solitary confinement, but I don't know the details.

In 1981, we were kept in the Under Eight[10] section of Ghezel Hesar Prison, and a woman named Anahita was kept in an unbelievably bad condition, chained to the front door. It was an excruciating scene. There was a former doctor named Mojgan (or Mojdeh) who ate nothing but dry bread

10 Under Eight is where the solitary confinement cells are located. The term Under Eight is used to refer to the part of a prison where prisoners are tortured, either by being kept in solitary confinement or physically abused.

and thought that instead of meat they put the flesh from the feet of the Taziri[11] prisoners in the food.

There were two sisters named Nadereh and Tahereh S. who were in Evin Prison in 1985. Tahereh had studied tele-communication engineering and Nadereh was a seventeen-year-old student. Tahereh had attempted suicide twice under intense pressure. Nadereh had become almost insane. She tore off all her clothes, stood under the lamp and twirled around. She would go to the bathroom and lie down. She always said that someone was talking to her. She wouldn't hurt anyone. In the middle of the night, she woke us up and said she wanted to talk about something she'd remembered.

A woman named Farzaneh was an agricultural engineer. I saw her in Ghezel Hesar in 1981. She was pregnant at the time and was later released. I was also released. When I was arrested again in 1985, I saw that Farzaneh had been arrested before me, but this time she had lost her sanity. She wouldn't go to the bathroom and was in a terrible condition.

Well, solitary confinement was tough. Time wouldn't move. In the cell, the only thing that calmed us down a bit was hearing the voices of other prisoners. There was also solidarity. When we were all flogged with cable, we had to endure the agonizing pain. We needed to talk.

We couldn't get out of the cramped area of the cell even to go to the toilet because it was in there with us. We weren't

11 *Tazir* offences are crimes for which there is no prescribed punishment in the Qur'an or hadith. Punishment is at the discretion of the state.

taken out for fresh air. I left the cell only for interrogation or to go to the bathroom, once a week for just a few minutes. We were constantly anxious, frightened of the male guards, and fretful hearing the voices of comrades being tortured in the interrogation rooms.

When was your next arrest and why did it happen?

I was arrested on 1 May 2011 at eight a.m. and was transferred to Ward 209. I entered cell 22 in the second corridor of the ward. When I was arrested, I had severe back pain and a sciatica problem. I writhed in agony on the floor. The cell was very dark. It was harder for me to put up with the situation compared to the previous times because now I was married and had a daughter. I kept thinking about Yasaman.

Yasaman was crying when I was arrested at home. They had difficulty convincing her to go to school. The hardest thing for me was leaving her. Later I heard that my husband, Mehdi, had become ill after my arrest.

Interrogations began the day after my arrest. A few days later I realized that my hearing was impaired and my voice wouldn't come out of my throat. The prison doctor said both were caused by nervous shock. I drank boiled water. They changed my cell. I was transferred to number 25, which was worse. It was smaller. The toilet was inside the cell and it was dark. It reminded me of my cell in 1985, where the toilet was inside. It was smothering to be in a cell which was so small that I could only walk three steps before hitting the wall.

From the beginning of my detention, I decided not to think about Yasaman, but I couldn't stop myself. All I could think about was what happened to Yasaman. I wished that I could hear about my daughter, but they would not allow me to call or have a meeting with her. I told my interrogator that I wouldn't speak until I heard from my daughter. It took three weeks for them to allow me to make a call.

Was the condition of your cell different from that of 1985?

The cell was small, dark and airless, like before. I didn't have my glasses and I couldn't see or read anything, not even the Qur'an. There was nothing but the Qur'an in that cell and I did not even read it. I had neither a pen nor paper. The loneliness was absolute and time did not pass. I was in that cell for two and a half months. I jumped up every time the irksome bell rang, even at night when I was asleep. Once I heard the voice of a mother imitating the voice of a child. At first, I thought they had brought a child to the ward, but then I realized what was going on.

Later I was taken to cell 12. The condition of the cell wasn't any different. It was even a little dimmer and it was a little bigger, but it was a big change for me and I was very thankful to God. To go to the toilet, we had to turn on the light button so that the female guards could come and take us. Going to and from the toilet and going to the bathroom for a few minutes a day made a little difference. When I was taken out for fresh air, the best thing about it was seeing the sky. I felt I was not alone, and it strengthened my spirits. I wore a chador when I was taken outside.

How long were you kept in solitary confinement?

I was in the cell for two and a half months. One day the female head of the ward came to my cell with a plastic cup of tea and said I had a guest. I felt my loneliness was about to end. A Christian woman became my cellmate. As she entered and removed the blindfold I went forward, hugged and kissed her. I apologized for doing it unexpectedly. I was very sad. I introduced myself and we started talking.

How was the food?

After a long time, they said that if we had money, we could buy fruit. When I was arrested, I had some money with me so I bought some, but I had lost seven kilos in the first week. I could not eat. I was shocked. I suffered from bleeding ulcers. The only thing I could have was a date with tea given to me in the morning and evening. It took me two or three weeks to get my voice right and I could not speak. In the interrogation room I had to drink hot water first to be able to speak a little.

How many times did they interrogate you during your time in solitary confinement?

I think I was interrogated twenty times in two months. The pressure in interrogation was high. They would give me clothes and tell me to get ready for the interview. During one of the interrogations, I lost my balance and was transferred to the ward's medical centre. A doctor was there, who they said was a neurologist. I couldn't stand on my feet. He put an anti-psychotic under my tongue. I felt like I couldn't control myself. I was lethargic for three days and could not speak.

Did you ever think that you might give up under the pressure of the interrogations and the difficult conditions of the cell?

When I was under pressure to do a TV interview, what devastated me was that they threatened my husband and especially my little girl. Once I got back to the cell after an interrogation full of threats and my fellow prisoners, Faran and Noushin, saw how shattered I was. The interrogators said that there were nine of us and everyone needed to be interviewed, and I had to be interviewed as well. Eventually, one night I said that I would do an interview just to get rid of the pressure of the interrogation and the cell. The day was decided, and I returned to the cell and did not sleep until four in the morning. I told Faran and Noushin that I had changed my mind – I wouldn't do an interview. But the interrogators wouldn't let me get away that easily.

When the warden came to get me the next morning, I asked her to tell the interrogators that I wouldn't come. When I was taken to the interrogation room they started yelling again. 'Are you toying with us?' they shouted. The pressure was too much because of the threats they made about Yasaman. Because of her, this time the situation was more difficult than the previous ones. Once I told them it was impossible for me to do an interview, I felt fearless in my heart. I was no longer afraid of anything. Their threats were absurd to me.

What did you do to strengthen your resistance?

I replayed the memories of the struggles of past generations in my mind. I thought of mothers who were killed for their children. I read the Qur'an. I thought that many mothers were separated from their children for their goals and ideals.

Every morning I exercised. When I was alone in the cell, I talked to myself in a voice that would have been heard from the next cell. I asked for a newspaper. I had no books. While I was alone in the cell, I felt extremely sad at sunset. Later when I shared the cell with two others, we asked for a TV set because we didn't know about current affairs.

Tell us about your little girl and how she coped.

In the cell, I thought that I had not been able to take care of my daughter properly, or as well as I should have. It broke my heart. I asked God for a chance to make amends. My first meeting with Yasaman took place about three months after my arrest. She did not raise her head. I was so eager to see her. I tried to pretend I was in good spirits. I kept telling her I was fine. Later I asked her why she didn't raise her head and look at me. She said she was afraid of crying. My daughter was very young, but she knew I was in a bad situation and I was fragile. This detention was not at all comparable to the previous two. This time I couldn't help but constantly think about my daughter.

How was the cell's hygiene?

Poor. The toilet was filthy. There was no separate place for washing clothes and I got a skin disease. The bathroom was filthy. I bought detergent and washed and cleaned it so that I could use it. We had to sweep the room with a small broom which was also broken.

I was not physically tortured during my arrest in 2011. This time it was psychological. In the 1980s I was tortured to confess things, but this time, although I was psychologically persecuted, no one asked me for information. They didn't want to investigate anything. They knew everything. Nonetheless, they kept us in the cell to confess.

NAZILA NOURI AND
SHOKOUFEH YADOLLAHI

Nazila Nouri (born 1968) and Shokoufeh Yadollahi (born 1967) are dervishes of the Ni'matullahi order. They were arrested on 20 February 2018 in Seventh Golestan Street, during a gathering of dervishes. The dervishes had gathered after security checkpoints had been set up on the street where Dr Nour-Ali Tabandeh,[1] the Qutb (spiritual leader) of the Ni'matullahi order, lived, amid the rumours of his possible arrest. About a hundred dervishes from the order were arrested and beaten by security forces, which meant they were already badly wounded and bleeding when they were then sent to solitary confinement.

---

1 Dr Nour-Ali Tabandeh was the spiritual leader of the Ni'matullahi (Sultan Ali Shahi) Gonabadi Order, the largest Sufi order in Iran. He died in 2019.

In the following interview Nazila and Shokoufeh speak about their experiences.

Nazila, what was the condition of your solitary confinement like and where were you imprisoned?

It was three o'clock in the morning when we were arrested. They kept us on the street until six a.m.

At seven, we arrived at Shapur Street Detention Centre. They kept the men there and took us to the Vozara Detention Centre. We were kept there until nightfall and were later transferred to Shahr-e Rey Prison.

Our clothes were bloody and soaking wet from the water cannons. We were left in these clothes. Others were transferred to cells with split heads and blood flowing from their wounds. Sepideh Moradi[2] was brought to a cell in Shahr-e Rey with swollen legs and other injuries. I had also been severely beaten, and my wrists were badly hurt. I was in excruciating pain and was bleeding from a blow to my head. Shokoufeh had also been struck on the head and her skull was fractured, but we were all transferred to three quarantine cells in this condition. The cells had no facilities. One of the cells was two by two meters, and

2 Sepideh Moradi is a dervish who was also arrested in 2018 following clashes with the security forces. She was sentenced in absentia to five years in prison.

there were three of us inside. The toilet inside that cell had no door or wall. It was a torment for us to use it in the presence of two other people in a small cell. The door to the cell was made of metal, with a small hatch. The toilet was clogged, and sewage water had overflowed. The cell reeked so much that we became nauseous. We covered our mouths and noses with our clothing to inhale a little less of the stench.

One of us who had asthma was so ill that she could not even breathe easily. She was taken to the hospital several times in a very bad condition but would return without receiving treatment in the same state as before. In one of the cells, the toilet had exuded so much sewage that it could no longer be used. A light above our heads was on day and night, and it was very dim, straining our eyes. It was so weak that we would have preferred to turn it off altogether.

Tell us more about the standard of hygiene.

In the bathroom, there was a shower just above the toilet, but it was impossible to stand there with the toilet blocked and the sewers overflowing. The toilet was so dirty that the stench bothered us all through the day and night. Even at night when we wanted to sleep, we would lift the collars of our blouses and wrap them around our mouths so that we might be able to rest. We asked the officers for detergents and disinfectants to at least clean the toilets, but they did not give us detergents or even a brush. The filth looked as if it had accumulated on the toilet for years and couldn't be cleaned. The drain was so backed up that we had to put a blanket in a garbage bag and put it on the toilet during non-use hours to get rid of the stench for a while. They didn't provide enough hygiene items for bathing either. When we entered the cell, they gave us a small bottle of shampoo. Our hair became rough like a scrub sponge and could no longer be combed. The water in Qarchak Prison[3] was the worst and saltiest water and bathing with it ruined our skin and hair.

Were you allowed any fresh air?

We were not taken out of the cell for ten days and we were under the light of that bulb. Then they started to take the prisoners out for fresh air. At first we were taken out for twenty minutes every day. Later it became thirty minutes.

How was the food?

In the first days they only gave us bread and halva. One of the detainees was diabetic and I heard her protest that she could not eat bread and flour every day. And so she was starving. After a few days they gave us small pieces of cheese and bread. We did not have drinking water and drank the

3 Infamous for its poor conditions, Tehran's Qarchak Prison holds 1,400 women, twice its capacity.

tap water, which was salty and not safe. We protested and asked for drinkable bottled water and even filed a complaint.

Were you interrogated?

Some of us were brought to Shapour Criminal Investigation Department for interrogation. Those who know Shapour Department know that it is one of the scariest and most difficult places to bring the accused. Several dervish men were tortured and beaten here in horrible ways. We were in Qarchak in solitary confinement cells that had four locks on their doors. We had no access to anything, and no communication was possible. One day, our fellow dervish Elham Ahmadi was taken out of the cell. We waited for her, but she wasn't brought back. The officers wouldn't tell us where she was no matter how many times we asked. She was returned to the cell two days and three nights later. We later found out that she had been taken to Shapour for questioning. Shapour's Department was so filthy. Those who were held there for some time suffered from infestations like lice. Of course, some of us were also interrogated in Qarchak Prison. Our interrogators came from two institutions: the Ministry of Intelligence and the Revolutionary Guards.

You were arrested together with your children. How did the arrest of your family members affect you?

My son Kiarash was arrested with me. He was twenty years old at the time. I was unaware of what was happening to him for a long time. My biggest concern was my son's condition. The first time they allowed me to call my husband, I just asked him to update me on Kiarash's condition. My son was shot and injured when he and I were arrested. The last picture I had of him was with very deep wounds, and much later I learned that Kiarash had been kept in Shapour cells for three months and had endured very terrible conditions. We were arrested in March 2018 and Kiarash had been kept in a cell for a month without even being allowed to change his clothes.

Nazila, you were alone in the cell for a while. Tell us about that period.

I underwent curettage at the hospital and when I was sent back to prison, I was transferred to another cell and left alone. There was a woman in the next cell who told me that women dervishes were being electrocuted in the hallway and she had seen it. My cell was four doors away from the hallway. I could hear the electric shock. When I was transferred from the hospital to the cell, I was still bleeding from the operation and I didn't feel well. I started protesting and asked them to at least give me water.

For two days I was not given any food or water, and no

one came to see me at all. I went on a dry hunger strike because I was furious about both the beating of the dervish prisoners who had started a sit-down hunger strike in the corridor and the way that the officers treated me.

I didn't feel well because I had just returned from the hospital and surgery. I needed care and hygiene, but they did not even give me soap and shampoo. I was left in a cell without any sanitary facilities. On the fourth day of the dry hunger strike, my fever rose sharply. I did not go to the hospital and I did not even allow them to take my temperature and blood pressure. The agents went to Shokoufeh and brought her to me with a glass of plain water to break my strike. I ended my strike and was kept in a cell for eleven days.

Shokoufeh, did you also go on a hunger strike in solitary confinement and in the public ward?

When we were taken out of the quarantine cells, we started a sit-in. We protested against not being allowed to make phone calls after months of solitary confinement. We asked that our demands be considered. The prison guards attacked us in a group. I saw for myself that Mr Pour-Abdul ordered the attack. The agents struck our heads and faces directly with an electric cattle prod. I had been electrocuted so much that I became completely numb. They shocked me from head to toe. Our clothes were all torn and we were severely beaten. That was why we decided to go on a hunger strike.

The other dervishes who were inside the cells did the same.

We went on a hunger strike for eighteen days but then broke it after a message from our friends outside the prison. During this time, our families mainly waited in front of the prison. They stood at the doors so as to see the officials and question them about our situation.

How were your visits?
We had a face-to-face meeting every three months.

Nazila, what kind of dress code did you have to follow?
When we were taken to Qarchak Prison, a chador was mandatory. So that the rest of the prisoners would not feel that we were a separate group, we agreed to wear a chador. One day I was called to go to the office of the head of the ward. I wore a coat and a scarf. The officer said that I was not allowed to go to see him without wearing a chador.

'It is what it is,' I told him, 'otherwise, I won't go.' And I went back to my bed. Eventually they had to accept, and I went with a coat and a scarf. Then one day they called me to see my family and I left without wearing a chador, again. The agents stopped me from going to the meeting room without a chador, so I went back to the cell. The officer came again and said that my family had come for a face-to-face visit after three months and told me to wear a chador and go. I said I would not go in a chador. Eventually, they agreed, and I went to see my family without wearing a chador.

Shokoufeh, tell us a little about how you felt in the cell and in quarantine.

I had been beaten on the head during the arrest and I had problems as a result. One was that I lost my sense of smell. My head injury got infected, and I had a fever. I felt terrible at night. I remember one night I couldn't sleep, so I got up in the middle of the night to pour a little warm water on my head so that I might feel a little better. It was hard, but I was trying to be good. The fact is that I had inner peace in the cell.

I was unaware of Dr Nour-Ali Tabandeh's condition and this concerned me. Not knowing about the conditions of my three sons was another of my worries. Kasra and Pouria were arrested because they were dervishes. Amir was not a dervish, but he was also arrested, and I was very upset that he'd been taken because of me and his brothers. I was worried about how the children would cope with this difficult situation. Kasra was sentenced to twelve years in prison, Amir to five years and Pouria to eight months. Kasra and Amir are still in prison.

Nazila: In the cell I felt that someone watched me all the time. I was alone and I had nothing but two blankets. The hygiene and cleanliness was appalling, but I felt good. I was worried about Kiarash. I became awfully worried when I heard that Kiarash had not been returned after he was first sent to the Greater Tehran Central Penitentiary and then taken out of it.

I had heard that he was under a lot of pressure to confess to false charges. When I called my husband, I'd tell him to find to Kiarash, lest he be tortured like Sattar Beheshti[4] and killed in solitary confinement. I was worried that he would be forced to confess to lies and be sentenced to death. Not knowing about Kiarash was the worst and most bitter period of my life. When I learned where he was after three months, I breathed a sigh of relief. On the night of my arrest, I had been forced to leave him while he was badly injured. I knew that despite his many injuries, he would still have to endure a lot of coercion and suffering.

Overall, I feel that during this period many things that were valuable to me outside prison don't matter to me any more, and things that I used to take for granted, such as walking on Pasdaran Street, are now endowed with a different meaning. Of course, Kiarash, who was sentenced to sixteen and a half years in prison, is still one of my biggest worries.

---

4 Seyyed Sattar Beheshti died in 2012, after being arrested by Iran's cyber police and complaining of torture in custody.

MARZIEH AMIRI

Marzieh Amiri Ghahfarrokhi is a journalist, student activist, political prisoner, women's rights activist and economics journalist for the Sharq *newspaper in Iran. Marzieh was arrested while following the situation of the detainees of the Labour Day rally in 2019 in the Arg area of Tehran. She had previously been arrested on 8 March 2018, along with dozens of others, for attending a ceremony marking International Women's Day.*

Marzieh was eventually sentenced by the Revolutionary Court of the Islamic Republic to ten years and six months in prison and 148 lashes, having to serve at least six years behind bars under Article 134 of the Islamic Penal Code of Iran.

She was temporarily released from Evin Prison on 26 October 2019 after posting bail.

How were you arrested and why were you transferred to solitary confinement?

I was arrested on 1 May, International Workers' Day, and I was immediately transferred to the Vozara Detention Centre. I spent the night in the same detention centre. There were about twelve of us who were put in two cells. The next day they took us to the courthouse. They took me from the courthouse to a place like a mosque or a *hosayniya*[1] (I'm not sure). I was there for about six hours. I had no idea where I was or what was going to happen except that I was in an empty hall and some men wearing masks came and went. A female guard would occasionally check on me and leave. From the very first minutes I protested, asking where I was and demanding the right to have phone calls, but of course no one answered. I started shouting. In response I only heard 'shut up woman', but half an hour later I was taken to a van and then to a detention centre which I learned belonged to Sarollah Camp. I was kept there for nine days. The cell had a toilet and bathroom, and was roughly three by three metres. It had a heavy door with a hatch. Of course, the door was always closed, except when food and tea were brought to us – then they would open the hatch and close it immediately.

1 A *hosayniya* is a congregational hall for Twelver Shia Muslim ceremonies, especially those mourning the martyrdom of Imam Hussain at Karbala.

What was the atmosphere like in the cell?
There was absolutely no sound in the ward. It was a terrible place for me, because I never knew if there was another prisoner besides me.

Where were you transferred to after nine days?
After nine days I was transferred to Ward 209. In 209 I was in solitary confinement for about twenty-eight days.

The cell was very small. It was about 120 by 180 centimetres. It was next to a bathroom with an iron door with a hatch. They left it open during the day. As I approached the toilet, I could hear the voices of the prisoners being taken to and from it. We were blindfolded in this cell as well, but blindfolds were not taken as seriously in Ward 209 as they were in Sarollah Camp. It was a piece of cloth and it was possible to play with it and not cover your eyes completely, but the blindfold of the previous detention centre was multilayered and covered almost half of my face, only my mouth was free.

What was the cell like?
It was small. There was a lamp inside that was always on. That damn lamp was so bright that sometimes I thought a sun was attacking my eyes with a razor.

The toilet and the bathroom were outside the cell and therefore I could get out of the cell for a moment. In Ward

209 there were writings on the walls. Sarollah Camp, however, was newly built, so no writings could be seen on the door or walls. No trace of anyone was seen on the cell wall. In Ward 209 writing on the walls was banned, but there were handwritten notes from previous prisoners on the walls anyway.

It was as if those notes gave you the addresses of previous occupants, people who were unfamiliar and unknown to you, and sometimes you could get to know each other. They were a means of communication, a pathway between the prisoner of today and the prisoner of yesterday which was very heart-warming.

What were the facilities inside the cell?

The cell had a small toilet but there was nothing else. Pens and paper were banned. When I entered the cell and they gave me the blankets, a pen fell out as I opened them. The previous prisoner must have hidden it so that it wouldn't fall into the hands of the officers and the next prisoner could use it.

How were the fresh air hour conditions?

In 209 we were taken out for fresh air three times a week, for twenty minutes each time. In Sarollah Camp it was thirty minutes every day. We had to wear hijab, a headscarf, a coat, trousers and chador. The walls were remarkably high around the space in Sarollah. Yellow flowers had grown in the narrow spaces between mosaics. My friend had talked to me about these yellow flowers and that they were the only things that reminded her of life during the time she was under arrest. From these flowers I realized that this was the place where my friend used to be. I felt that I was not alone; Parisa was there with me.

How were the hygiene and bathroom conditions?

I went to the bathroom three times a week. Once a week they would give you a vacuum cleaner so that you could clean your cell.

How did the cell and the solitude affect you?

Being left alone in a closed environment is horrible for everyone and I am no exception. You are alienated from every feature of human life. You are questioned about everything during the interrogations. You are addressed only by the interrogator and when you are taken back to the cell, you're all alone. Solitude in a cell is different from solitude outside. There's no one in a cell besides you. You want to talk but you can't. There are moments when you feel the walls are approaching you. You feel the walls are moving towards each other and you're being crushed under their pressure. It was a very strong feeling that actually made me short of breath.

I remember one day in Sarollah Camp, the female guard came to my cell and told me to wear a chador because someone was coming to see me. A man with a mask on his face unexpectedly appeared in the doorway and told me to sit. He sat in front of me. What he said didn't matter as I didn't listen to him. But it was excruciating and agonizing for me that the solitude of the cell had disappeared only by 'this man's' presence.

How did you entertain yourself in the cell?

There was nothing for entertainment. You could only wrestle with your mind. I sometimes imagined myself in the company of my friends and I talked to them. I tried to talk about subjects other than the prison so that I wouldn't be disconnected from the world outside.

On the days when you're taken to interrogation you are at least doing something. When there was no interrogation, time would be entirely forgotten. It wouldn't pass. I tried to sleep to pass the day and reach the night, but I had no factual understanding of whether it was day or night. I didn't know when the day ended. There's really nothing in solitary confinement to mark the time.

Before I was imprisoned, I sometimes used to sit for hours and think, in a bus stop for instance. Or I'd lie for two hours and just think thoughts without any purpose, but in solitary confinement there is nothing to stimulate your mind. Sometimes you even try to remember and review things from the past, but at some point you get sick and tired of this struggle. These are very sad moments. Sometimes you can't even remember the important events of your life. It's like looking for something in a crowded and cluttered place without finding it.

In solitary confinement all contact with friends, family and the environment is completely cut off. How did you cope with this?

I exercised a lot. I'd do the exercises that I already knew, danced a lot, made various gestures with my face and body, and I laughed a lot at this game that I had started with myself. I wanted to talk to someone – someone other than the interrogator, of course. In the cell, it's only the officer who opens the door. The prisoner goes to the toilet and the bathroom and returns. In this very simple incident, two sentences may be exchanged between the prisoner and the officer, but a human relationship formed between the guard and me.

When a prison guard enters the ward or changes shifts with her colleagues, the clothes she wears are an objective reminder of the life that goes on outside those walls. Most female guards were not ideologically motivated. They were the salaried staff who carried out their duties of monitoring the prisoner. A young prison guard, perhaps less experienced, had a judgmental demeanour, but there were also older women who were more experienced and patient. Basically, they did not treat us with the prevailing ideological prejudice. In encounters with some of the female guards, I would say in my heart, 'Have you been taken captive too?' When the guards changed shifts, the change of officers and the change of faces in the ward gave me a sense of being alive. Of course, it would pain me that the prison had been able to diminish my delights and views to this, but anyway these encounters and feelings did matter. Facing the interrogator, however, I felt different; they always sought to reprimand me, and nothing but anger and hatred settled in me.

Do you think that the behaviour of the prison guards is related to the interrogators' orders?

Whenever I heard footsteps outside my cell, I would get up to see the person passing by through the hatch. One day a guard was standing by the door. She suddenly opened the door and warned me that if I did that again, she would close the hatch on the door. When a cellmate was brought to my cell, the same officer, who had not even allowed me to look through the hatch, would now stop and speak a little. I asked her why it was that when I was alone in the cell, she had never talked to me, but now that the interrogator had ordered another person to share my cell, she talked to me. She denied it, but it was true.

The way in which a human being was held in a small cell and the way the guards treated the prisoner indicated that these things had been carefully calculated. For example, when a prisoner was taken out of solitary confinement, then the guards treated her better and exchanged a few sentences.

What was the atmosphere like in the interrogation cells and, as the saying goes, how was the game played?

In Sarollah Camp we were blindfolded when we were taken from the cell to the interrogation room which was a very short distance.

The female guard took me to the interrogation room. Sometimes she would sit in the room, and sometimes she would leave when the interrogator arrived. I was blindfolded during the interrogation. I was allowed to lift the blindfold a little when I was asked to write, so that I could see the paper. Interrogations took place in different prisons, and in the morning, at noon, or at night. The first day of interrogation started at about eight p.m. and went on for about six hours. At Sarollah Camp, the interrogator wrote the questions and there was no talking. It was just writing. During these sessions the interrogator blamed me for everything.

In Ward 209, however, I took off my blindfold during the interrogation and could see the interrogator's face. In 209 the interrogator discussed many events, including social issues. There was no such atmosphere in Sarollah Camp. On the contrary, the interrogator would get very involved in my personal life, for example, about whether I was single or married, whether I was with someone or not, who came to my house and why, and asked different questions about my travels or, for example, my mobile phone. He checked my phone at the same time, as the interrogation went on. I was questioned about it there, but in 209 they did not bring the phone to interrogation sessions. They checked the phone beforehand and then questioned me during the session.

Did they tell you about how long you would have to serve when convicted?

The interrogators said from the beginning that I would be sentenced to ten to fifteen years.

Did they pressure you through pressuring your family?

My family members tried not to let my mother know that I had been arrested. The interrogator threatened to bring my mother there to see me in my prison clothes. Or he threatened to call my mother and say I was in prison. Sometimes they threatened to arrest my sister. They didn't allow me to call her until I said I wouldn't want to contact anyone but my sister, and if they wouldn't allow that then I wouldn't call my family at all.

Did you need medical care and did you receive it?

I felt better in Sarollah, but my blood pressure would frequently drop. It was constantly low. They blindfolded me twice and checked my blood pressure. A very superficial examination was done. It had not been long since I had been detained in Ward 209, and my transfer was stressful. The interrogations were long and the solitary confinement wound me up mentally and physically.

I had epilepsy, and of course I was worried about my illness. I had told and written to the interrogator many times, but he did not pay any attention. One day I was in solitary confinement and when I got up, I lost consciousness. I had had a seizure. I'd fallen to the ground. I was still alone in the cell when I regained consciousness. My body was shaking so much that I held my legs with my hands. I stayed in this position until I got a little better and was able to stand. I called and the prison officer came. I explained what had happened. He said that the prison authorities had said they would take me to the doctor.

It took me a long time to get to the doctor. My heart rate was very high and my blood pressure was very low. He gave me an Inderal pill and they sent me back to the cell. I had epilepsy for many years before my arrest, but there were long intervals between my seizures. The last time it happened had been three years before. I did not have palpitations outside at all. I had not had any digestive trouble when I was free and I had not even taken a single pill for it before, but now I had a stomach ulcer in prison. When I was taken to the hospital, the doctor said the prison conditions had given me the ulcer.

Were you allowed to see your family and make phone calls?

I wasn't allowed to meet my family in the first weeks. During the last two weeks of interrogation, I had two meetings with my family. It was also possible to make calls once a week. Indeed, I could make a phone call only after an interrogation. Early on, the interrogator stood over me, so I was very stressed while talking to my family, but past a certain point I resolved to ignore the interrogator. After that I felt good about the phone calls. I was better off hearing a voice asking me how I felt and showing compassion, instead of reprimanding me and holding me accountable

When I was removed from that place of interrogation, I felt hope that I was not the person the interrogators said I was and wanted me to be. The atmosphere of interrogation and solitude in solitary confinement is like a space that keeps you away from everything. The interrogator wants you to feel guilty. You even blame yourself for your thoughts. They want to change you into someone you're not. In fact, the interrogator wants to put you in a situation where you think you are living a public lie. Overcoming what is being imposed on you is a constant struggle and only this can save you.

What were your most painful moments and experiences inside the cell?

There were two. When I was in solitary confinement, an officer came and said, 'I'm going to change your cell.' I got up and they took me to a cell with two other cellmates. It was very strange. I could talk. I could eat. Without knowing them, without any connection between us, it felt good to be with people in a similar situation. I told myself that at least my loneliness was over.

The next day I was taken back to solitary confinement. I stayed until one day they came and took me to another cell with two other people. This time, when I was in the cell with them, I was anxious lest it happen again. Two days later, I was returned to solitary confinement. I felt terrible. I banged my hand on the wall. At that moment I saw myself as mad, and I experienced a fear that was not the fear of the interrogator and the prison – I feared myself. I banged my hand harshly against the wall. I wanted to feel the physical pain. Your bedrock is the principle of social life, and the solitary cell takes it all away from you. In solitary confinement you can neither speak nor hear a sound. Even if you hear footsteps approaching, you should ignore them. You have to stay within the constraints that the interrogator has set for you and accept that you are in solitary confinement.

You do not see or hear anyone or anything except the image and sound of the interrogator. The interrogator automatically becomes important to you. He is the one who can lead you to the abyss of destruction, but at the same time insinuates to you that he is the only one who can save you, an entity who is there to accuse and punish you. This entity is the only one who talks to you and you talk to him.

How did you resist and what factors helped to increase your resistance?

Thinking and wanting to live was the most important and biggest support for me. When I was frustrated with everything, I thought I could create real hope in the moment and connect my past to the future. This desire also helped me not be intimidated by the interrogator and my situation. Believing that my life was going on helped me to continue living, not just being interrogated. The recollections I had heard of former prisoners came to life in my cell. I thought about how they had also lived and resisted in this cell. My head was full of their resistance, resilience and steadfast resolution. The fact is, of course, that the conditions and characteristics of solitary confinement are so difficult that they are constantly at odds with something called 'strong will'. Sometimes you forget the meaning of this idea completely, because you've merely heard it as a general and prescriptive conceptual idea.

When the interrogator tells you to get a roommate when you're released from prison, when he talks about daily chores as the inquisition goes on to remind you of life outside prison, he's flaunting his power to deprive you of life. The interrogator tries his best to crush you in any way. In these moments, only the birth of an inner power will give you continued sustenance, a power that is unique to these conditions. Until this point, you had been unaware of the existence and emergence of such a power. It is something that helps you stand up to the status quo. In fact, in these circumstances you strive for survival, and perhaps nothing but survival can push you forward.

The interrogator tries to take you away from all human values. In addition to the walls hemming in your body, he tries to constrain your psyche, so resistance also occurs in the mind. The interrogator tries to subject your mind to his domination without you realizing it. Even an insight into how this system works is obtained very slowly, an insight that can help you resist. Before being detained you have a narrative of yourself and your existence that you craft from your experience and presence in society. Now, not only are you suddenly reprimanded and found guilty by the interrogator for aspects of your individual and community identities, but you are also told a false account of yourself for which you should be punished. The spirit of repression that you have experienced in various ways in your family and society is now in front of you, unmasked and naked.

In the mind of the interrogated person, nothing is as strong as fear. Everything from blindfolds to the wall in front of you being half a metre away, to the presence of heavy bodies sitting behind you, encircling you with questions like a mechanical machine and pushing you into a tight spot, is terrifying. All of this is arranged in such a way that it insinuates to you that you are a wrongdoer so that you are engulfed by fear, but in these moments there is an incredible living will in the human being that can grow and progress.

Sometimes my brain or conscious will stopped resisting, but something deep inside my body or soul, proud of my broken self, pushed me to keep resisting.

The feeling of fear is the background of all the days spent in the cell. Fear, reprimand, punishment, isolation, intimidation, deprivation and coercion are things that are strongly imposed on you in detention, but you have already experienced that as the logic behind all politics as a woman before your arrest, or you have heard from other women's experiences. This situation had been imposed on me as a woman by my father, brother and the patriarchal system that governed me. It has a logic that sees itself as the master, or at least as the one with the right to take away your choice and decide your destiny.

In prison, the interrogator is not merely an interrogator, but a representative of the patriarchal order that silences your voice if you refuse to do what he wants. In this system, you can have a legitimate presence, be seen or respected, but only if you are tame, obedient and committed to maintaining and enforcing the existing order. I borrow a sentence from Reza Baraheni[2] here: 'Is it possible to trust someone who has two kinds of language, two kinds of voice, who beats you with one language and with the other gently and calmly deprives

2 Reza Baraheni is an exiled Iranian novelist who lives in Canada.

you of liberty and willpower? Can one consider oneself contemptible and the other great? Is it possible for you to consider yourself forbidden and the other allowed, and as a result, victorious? Or can one see obedience as the only way to survive?' These sentences are very inspiring to me.

Such an order wants to make it clear to others that some can and are allowed to command and deny others because they have more power, while others are powerless and inferior. The common denominator between the interrogation context and patriarchal society can be seen here. Through inquisition, violence and punishment, an interrogator plays the same role as father, brother, husband and state who enforce a process of othering when dealing with women.

Without any intention to compare men and women and based only on the stories I have heard from female prisoners in our enlightening conversations, I think that what women have endured through their lived experience allows them to see the oppression imposed on them under interrogation as less alien. The interrogator's gendered shift in approach that women experience is as strong as their resistance. 'I don't know why it's so hard to interrogate girls', an interrogator once said to me, 'and why they constantly quarrel with their interrogators.'

It may have been said with masculine desire or it may have been a superficial and pointless joke, but to me it was meaningful. A woman sitting in an interrogation chair may consciously or unconsciously tell herself the truth as it's a situation she has experienced before or at least is familiar with. 'I am against the order that appoints you as my inquisitor and guard, and defines me as your subordinate. I am against inequality.'

A woman's lived experience helps her. The 'strong will' I talked about has different meanings for interrogated people in relation to the oppression they have experienced. The caring characteristic that has historically been entrusted to women is a good guide to building a 'strong will' in a feminine way. Under the conditions of interrogation, this familiar characteristic of women's morale can make it possible for her inner sense of responsibility to emerge. Then she will take care of herself and of those who are emotionally and politically close to her. In an unequal situation of one person dominating, you either have to follow or be dominated. In the highly unequal and unjust situation created by the interrogator, a woman who herself has been wounded by a more generally unequal situation can develop resistance that is rooted in her daily experience.

She can now take care of those whom she considers her family, not to prove to them that she is 'strong', but to worry about them, now that she is forced to sit in the interrogation chair. I would like to say that the common literature of the interrogation narrative has a 'strong will', what I see as 'failure' of men's literature. On the one hand, this literature's ideal role model is a hero who does not complain under any given circumstance, and on the other hand, for the sake of slandering the other man (the sovereignty), it leaves untold any kind of real and human narrative of the suffering and doubt of the interrogated person. Because the big bully should not know that for a moment we may 'fail to be strong'! Women's literature about being in prison and under interrogation may not be looking for a hero, a Rostam.[3] Instead of denying and glamourizing the suffering caused by the unequal and cruel interrogation situation, the desire to live freely alleviates her suffering and gives her the strength to continue. With respect to all egalitarian men and women, I think the model of interrogation and even the narrative of the experience of interrogation and imprisonment of activist men differs from that of activist women, and gender can provide a good reason for this difference.

In masculine culture, and consequently in its hierarchical politics, the man seeks superiority. When he is pushed down the hierarchy, he displays more fragility because his authority is suddenly undermined and weakened, leaving him in a vulnerable situation. The woman, however, is already in this inferior position and declares her existence by her rebellion and disobedience. In the same way, a woman's mere presence in the interrogation cell already means victory. Anchored by her feminine experience, she can never trust someone who has two languages and two voices.

3 Rostam is a legendary hero in Persian mythology known in folklore for being invincible.

POSTSCRIPT: UPDATES ON THE WOMEN INTERVIEWED

Nigara Afsharzadeh

A citizen of Turkmenistan who was imprisoned in Iran on charges of espionage, she returned to her country and spent time in prison there as well. She has now been released and lives in Turkmenistan with her two children.

Atena Daemi

A human rights activist she was sentenced to six and a half years in prison. Following her release on the completion of her sentence, she lives with her family in Tehran.

Zahra Zahtabchi

Charged with membership of the People's Mojahedin Organization of Iran. Sentenced to ten years in prison, which she is still serving.

Mahvash Shahriari

A member of the Yaran committee of the Bahá'ís of Iran, she was released in 2017 after serving her ten-year jail sentence. In 2017 she was named the International Writer of Courage by PEN and was a co-winner of the Pinter Prize for a volume of her prison poetry, now translated into several languages. Amid a widespread attack on the members of the Bahá'í community, Mahvash was arrested on 31 July 2022 and is currently held in custody on charges of spying.

Hengameh Shahidi

Her complaints regarding corruption in the judiciary resulted in her receiving a thirteen-year prison sentence. She spent seventeen months in solitary confinement followed by fifteen months in prison. She was released in 2021, subsequent to protests and appeals to the Supreme Leader's office. She is still receiving medical treatment to address the damage caused by solitary confinement and has not been able to resume her normal life.

Reyhaneh Tabatabai

Member of an Iranian reformist political party (Union of Islamic Iran People), she was released from prison in 2016. She currently serves as the chief editor of *Emtedad News*.

Sima Kiani

A member of the Bahá'í community, she was sentenced to five years in prison of which four years are suspended. She lives in Tehran.

Fatemeh Mohammadi

Fatemeh is a Christian convert. She was arrested in 2017 and charged with national security crimes, Christian activities and being a member of a missionary group. She received a six-month prison sentence and was released upon its completion. She was arrested for a second time in 2020 for taking part in protests against Ukraine International Airline Flight PS752 being shot down by the Islamic Revolutionary Guard Corps. She was sentenced to three months in jail and ten lashes. She is prohibited from attending university. Due to intervention by the Ministry of Intelligence, she has not been able to find employment.

Sedigheh Moradi

Charged with membership of the People's Mojahedin Organization of Iran, she was released from jail in 2016. She was rearrested again in 2019 and spent three months in solitary confinement in Ward 209. She is currently free.

Nazila Nouri

A member of the Sufi dervish community of Iran, she was sentenced to one year in jail. She was released in 2019 and practises her profession as a medical doctor.

Shokoufeh Yadollahi

A member of the Sufi dervish community of Iran, her five-year prison sentence was reduced to two years on appeal. She was released in 2020.

Marzieh Amiri

A journalist, a student rights and women's rights activist. She was sentenced to ten years in prison which was reduced to five years on appeal. She spent seven months in jail and was released in 2019. She is working as a journalist.

INDEX

Abbasi, Judge Pir 145
Abrahamian, Ervand 3
Afkari, Navid xxxi–xxxii
Afsharzadeh, Nigara 1, 51–62, 229
Aftab magazine 43
Ahari, Shiva Nazar 37
Ahmadi, Elham 203
Ahmadi, Seyyed Bahram Resteh 46–7, 48–9
Ahmadzadeh Heravi, Taher 19, 175
Aksariat Organization 190
Alawi, Mr 82, 85, 86–8
Amadnews 146
American Physical Society xxxiv
Amiri, Marzieh 209–27, 232
Amnesty International xxii, xxvi
Anaraki, Rahimipour 10

anti-government demonstrations xv, xxviii
anxiety 7, 8, 27–8, 100–1
Ardabili Court 26
arrests xxviii, xxx, xxxii, 15
  and Afsharzadeh 51–2, 58, 60
  and Amiri 209, 210
  and Daemi 63, 65, 68, 69, 73–7
  and Kiani 167, 168
  and Mohammedi, Fatemeh 175
  and Mohammadi, Narges xiii, xxi, xxii–xxiv, xxv–xxvi, xxvii, 16, 26–7, 40–1
  and Moradi 183, 193
  and Nouri/Shokoufeh 204
  and Nouri/Yadollahi 199
  and Shahidi 137, 143–4, 145–6

and Shahriari 113
and Tabatabai 157–8,
160–1, 162
and Zaghari-Ratcliffe 92
and Zahtabchi 75–6, 81, 82,
83, 85, 86
Asgari, Amir Hossein
(Mahdavi) 142, 144
Ashton, Catherine xxvii
Ashura 73, 159, 161
Association for the Defence of
Rights of Prisoners xxxiii
Azima, Parnaz 144

Bahá'í community 2, 130–1,
230, 231
and Kiani 167, 174
and Shahriari 113–14, 115
Bahar (newspaper) 164
Bahá'u'lláh 120, 171–2
Baniasadi, Mr 18
Baqiyatallah Hospital 21, 74
Baraheni, Reza 224
bathing facilities 19
and Afsharzadeh 53–4
and Amiri 213
and Daemi 70–1
and Mohammadi, Fatemeh
176–7
and Moradi 198
and Shahidi 139–40, 149
and Zaghari-Ratcliffe 94
Bauer, Shane 37

Bazargan, Mehdi 30
Bazargan, Ozra xxix
beatings xvi, xxix–xxx
Behbahani, Simin xxxiv
Beheshti, Sattar xxvi–xxvii, 208
blindfolds 7
and Afsharzadeh 52, 53, 56
and Amiri 211, 217
and Kiani 170
and Mohammadi, Fatemeh
179
and Mohammadi, Narges
16, 17, 18, 24
and Shahriari 115
and Zaghari-Ratcliffe 98
and Zahtabchi 79
British Foreign Office xxvi,
103

Camp Ashraf 84
Center for Women's
Citizenship xxxiv
Change for Equality
Campaign xxxiv
children 4, 9–10, 30, 137, 204
and Afsharzadeh 51–2,
57–8, 59
and Moradi 193, 194, 197,
198
see also Rahmani, Ali;
Rahmani, Kiana;
Ratcliffe, Gabrielle
Christianity 175, 180, 181, 231

civil rights xxxiii–xxxv, 5
clothing 24, 149, 159, 165, 206–7
Committee for Defence of Free, Fair, and Safe Elections xxxiii
Committee for the Protection of Votes 30
conspiracy, *see* national security
Cotler, Irwin xxvi
Council of Nationalist-Religious Activists 15
Covid-19 pandemic xv, xxii, xxx, 5

Da (Hosseini) 164
Dadkhah, Seyed Mohammad Ali 31
Daemi, Atena 1, 63–74, 229
Danby, Michael xxvi
Davood, Haj 184–5
death penalty xxvii, xxxi–xxxii
Defenders of Human Rights Center (DHRC) xv, xvi, xxi, xxii, xxv, xxxiii
and interrogation 10, 25, 30–2
and solitary confinement xxxii
Dehnavi, Hassan Zare, *see* Haddad, Judge
democracy xxiii
dervishes 199–208, 232

Djalali, Ahmadreza xxxi–xxxii

Ebadi, Shirin xxxiv, 30, 31
Eid 76
Emtedad News 230
Engineering Inspection Corporation xxiii, xxv
Enlightening Youth Association xxxiii
espionage allegations 25, 51, 56–7, 91, 96, 229
ethnic minorities 4
Ettela'at (newspaper) 164
European Union (EU) xxvii
Evin Prison xiii, xv–xvi, xviii, xxv–xxvi, xxvii–xxix, xxxii
and Afsharzadeh 51, 52–61
and Daemi 63–74
and Kiani 168–74
and Mohammadi, Fatemeh 175–81
and Mohammadi, Narges 23–4, 41
and Moradi 183–98
and Shahidi 138–55
and Shahriari 114, 128–36
and Tabatabai 157–66
and Zaghari-Ratcliffe 91, 104–12
and Zahtabchi 76–90
execution 5, 30
extremists xxxv

family xvii, xxviii, 3, 4, 8, 9
    and Afsharzadeh 59
    and Amiri 218, 220
    and Daemi 69, 73–4
    and Kiani 168, 169
    and Mohammadi, Narges
        xxx, 10
    and Nouri/Shokoufeh
        206
    and Shahidi 148, 154
    and Shahriari 123–4, 132,
        133–5
    and Zaghari-Ratcliffe 95–6,
        100, 105–7, 108
    and Zahtabchi 75–6, 77, 82,
        85–9
    see also children
Fattal, Joshua 37
feminism xxiii
food xviii–xix, 7
    and Daemi 68
    and Mohammadi, Narges
        22, 29
    and Moradi 195
    and Nouri/Shokoufeh
        202–3
    and Shahriari 124
    and Tabatabai 159
    and Zaghari-Ratcliffe 94,
        108
    and Zahtabchi 81
    see also hunger strikes
France xxiv

Freedom Movement of Iran
    15, 18, 19
fresh air:
    and Afsharzadeh 53
    and Amiri 212–13
    and Daemi 68
    and Kiani 172
    and Mohammadi, Fatemeh
        177
    and Mohammadi, Narges
        22, 28, 46
    and Moradi 195
    and Nouri/Shokoufeh 202
    and Shahidi 149–50
    and Shahriari 124
    and Tabatabai 158, 166
    and Zaghari-Ratcliffe 112
    and Zahtabchi 78
Friends of Iran 129

Germany xxxiv
Ghahfarrokhi, Marzieh Amiri
    1
Gharavi, Dr 18
Ghasemzadeh, Bizhan 145
Ghezel Hesar Prison 146,
        184–5, 191–2
Gogol, Hassan 36
Golroo, Mahdieh 73
Green Movement 39, 161, 162
Guild of Journalists xxxiii

Haddad, Judge 15, 16, 21

Hajiloo, Mr 105–6
Halvaei Asgar, Mojtaba 184
healthcare xvii–xviii, 5
    and Afsharzadeh 54
    and Amiri 219–20
    and Daemi 74
    and Mohammadi, Fatemeh
        180–1
    and Mohammadi, Narges
        33–7, 39–40, 44, 45–6
    and Shahidi 152, 230
    and Zaghari-Ratcliffe 101,
        109
    and Zahtabchi 79–80
Hoodfar, Homa 107
Hosseini, Seyyedeh Zahra 164
hostages 3
human rights xxiii, xxxiv, 2,
        4–5, 89; see also Defenders
        of Human Rights Center
Human Rights Watch xxii
hunger strikes xxviii, 145,
        147–8, 205–6
hygiene, see bathing facilities;
        toilet facilities

insulting the leadership 63,
        137
interrogation 4, 8, 9–10
    and Afsharzadeh 55–60,
        61–2
    and Amiri 216, 217–18, 220,
        222–7

    and Daemi 68–9, 71–3
    and Kiani 168–71, 172–4
    and Mohammadi, Fatemeh
        178–80, 181
    and Mohammadi, Narges
        20–1, 22, 24–7, 29–33, 42
    and Moradi 190, 193, 196–7
    and Nouri/Shokoufeh 203
    and Shahidi 140–3, 144, 146
    and Shahriari 115, 121, 128,
        130–1
    and Tabatabai 159–60,
        161–2, 163
    and Zaghari-Ratcliffe 95,
        96–8, 99–100, 103, 110–11
    and Zahtabchi 77, 85–9
IRGC, see Islamic
        Revolutionary Guard
        Corps
Ishratabad Military Detention
        Centre 20, 43, 183–4
Islamic Iran Participation
        Front 157
Islamic Revolutionary Guard
        Corps (IRGC) xxviii, 15,
        63, 231
    and Tabatabai 157, 158, 163
    and Zaghari-Ratcliffe 104,
        105
isolation, see solitary
        confinement

Jalalian, Zeynab 38–9

Jalili, Saeed 144, 157
Jamali, Mr 26

Kachuei, Mohammad 184
Kaleme 161–2
Kamalabadi, Fariba 129, 132
Karaj 184
Karroubi, Mehdi 139, 140, 141
Kazemi-Ahmadabadi, Zahra
     'Ziba' xxvi, 35
Kerman Prison 91, 92–104
Khatami, Sayyid Mohammad
     138–9, 140, 141
Kiani, Sima 1, 167–74, 231
Kianmanesh, Mr 26, 27
Kirk, Mark xxvi
Kurdistan 38, 39

Lahidji, Shahla xxxiv
Larijani, Sadegh 151
lashes xiii–xiv, 209
LEGAM (Campaign for Step
     by Step Abolition of the
     Death Penalty) xxvii,
     xxxiii–xxxiv
light control 6–7

MacShane, Denis xxvi
Mafatih al-Jinan (Abbas Qumi)
     80, 102, 163
Mashhad 51, 58, 145
     and Shahriari 113, 115–17,
     134

men 3, 9
MI6 138, 141
Ministry of Intelligence xiii,
     xvi–xvii
   and Kiani 170
   and Mohammadi, Fatemeh
     231
   and Mohammadi, Narges
     23–4, 31, 39–40, 41–2
   and Moradi 183
   and Shahidi 138–9, 141–2,
     143, 146
   and Tabatabai 163
   and Zahtabchi 75
mirrors 60, 68, 74, 109–10, 135
Mofidi, Badralsadat 37
Mohammadi, Fatemeh (Mary)
     1, 175–81, 231
Mohammadi, Narges xiii, xiv,
     xv–xx, xxi–xxxiii, 1, 2
   and first incarceration
     15–22
   and second incarceration
     23–40
   and significance xxxiii–xxxv
   and third incarceration
     40–9
   and white torture 7, 9, 10
moharebeh (waging war against
     God) 82, 87
Mohebbi, Mr 27
Mohtashamipour,
     Fakhrossadat 161

Montazeri, Ayatollah 87
Moradi, Sedigheh 1, 183–98,
    231
Moradi, Sepideh 200
Moradi, Soraya 190–1
Mujahedin-e-Khalq 75–6, 84,
    184, 229, 231

Nahj al-Balagha 80–1
Na'impour, Mr 19
National Council of Peace
    xxxiii, 30
national security xxv, xxvii, 9,
    27, 30, 137
Neyssari, Afarin 108, 112
Nikou, Seyed Javad
    Khoshniyat 75, 76, 77, 85
Ni'matullahi order 199
Nirenstein, Fiamma xxvi
Nobel Women Initiative xxii
Nouri, Nazila 1, 199–208,
    232
Nowruz 145, 171, 172

Observatory for the Protection
    of Human Rights
    Defenders xxii
One Million Signatures
    Campaign to Change
    Discriminatory Laws
    xxxiv

Pahlavi dynasty 3–4

PEN International xxii, 136,
    230
People's Mojahedin
    Organization, *see*
    Mujahedin-e-Khalq
physiological effects 7–8
politics 4
Pour-Abdul, Mr 205
prisoners of conscience xix,
    xxxii–xxxiii; *see also*
    Mohammadi, Narges
propaganda against the regime
    (*nezam*) xxv, xxvii, 158,
    167, 175
    and Mohammadi, Narges
    26, 30

Qalibaf, Mohammed Baqer
    157
Qarchak Prison xiv, 202–8
Qazvin xxxiii
quarantine xvii, 47–8, 93,
    117–18
Qur'an 80, 81, 90, 97, 102
    and Moradi 188, 189, 194,
    197
    and Tabatabai 160, 163

Radio Farda 144
Rah-e Kargar 190
Rahmani, Ali 23, 26, 29, 32–3,
    37–8, 42–3
    and Zanjan 40, 41, 49

Rahmani, Kiana 23, 26, 29,
    32–3, 37–8, 42–3
  and Zanjan 40, 41, 49
Rahmani, Taghi xxiii–xxiv,
    15, 21, 22
  and exile xxv, xxx, 40, 41
Raja Shahr Prison xxxii
Rajaei, Alireza 20
Ramadan 108
Ratcliffe, Gabrielle (Gisoo) 91,
    95–6, 97, 99, 100, 102,
    106–7, 108, 112
Ratcliffe, Richard 91, 96, 97,
    100, 111, 112
*Reforms, the Strategy, and the
    Tactics, The*
    (Mohammadi) xxiii
Rejali, Darius M. 3
religious minorities 4, 5; *see
    also* Bahá'í community;
    Christianity
Reporters Without Borders
    xxii, xxvi
resistance 4–5
Revolutionary Court 145, 209
  Branch 4: 26
  Branch 15: 137
  Branch 26: 15–16, 175
  Branch 28: 183
Rezanezhad, Amir 8, 11
rule of law xxiii

Sabbaghian, Mr 18

Saber, Firoozeh 20
Saber, Hoda 16
Sagduni 115–17, 119–21
Sahabi, Ezzatollah 30
Salavati, Abolqasem 76, 81–2,
    86, 137, 151
sanctions 5
Sarollah Camp 159, 210,
    212–20
Sefat, Mehdi Khawas 183
Seifzadeh, Mohammad 31
sensory deprivation, *see* white
    torture
Shahid Moghaddas
    Prosecutor's Office
    46–7
Shahidi, Hengameh 1, 137–55,
    230
Shahr-e Rey 167, 168, 200
Shahriari, Mahvash 1, 113–36,
    230
Shi'a Islam 4
Shourd, Sarah 37
sit-down strikes xv–xvi, xxviii
smell 7
solitary confinement xix,
    xxxii–xxxiii, 8, 9
  and Afsharzadeh 52–3,
    54–5, 60–1, 62
  and Amiri 210–17, 221–3
  and Daemi 64–7, 69–70, 74
  and Jalalian 38–9
  and Kiani 168–70, 171–2

and Mohammadi, Fatemeh
176, 178, 180–1
and Mohammadi, Narges
xiii, xiv, 16–18, 20, 21–2,
25–6, 27–9, 37–8, 42–6
and Moradi 185–90, 191–8
and Nouri/Shokoufeh
200–1, 204–5, 207–8
and Shahidi 138, 139,
143–5, 147–8, 150–5
and Shahriari 114, 115–17,
122–3, 126–7, 131–4
and Tabatabai 158–9, 162–6
and Zaghari-Ratcliffe 91,
92–5, 96–7, 99–102
and Zahtabchi 75, 76, 78–9,
80–1, 83–5, 89–90
Soltani, Abdolfattah 31
Souri, Hojjatollah 185
Stop Execution of the Child
xxxiii
student activism xxiii
Sweden xxxiv

Tabandeh, Dr Nour-Ali 199,
207
Tabatabai, Reyhaneh 1,
157–66, 230
Tajzadeh, Sayyid Mostafa 161
*Tashakkol Daaneshjuyi
Roshangaraan* ('Enlighted
Student Group') xxiii,
xxxiii

Tavakoli, Mr 123
Tavassoli, Mr 18
Tehran 40–1; *see also* Evin
Prison
telephone calls xviii
and Afsharzadeh 59
and Amiri 220
and Daemi 73
and Shahidi 148
and Shahriari 132
and Zaghari-Ratcliffe 96,
102, 105–6
and Zahtabchi 77
Thomson Reuters Foundation
91
toilet facilities 18–19
and Afsharzadeh 53
and Daemi 70–1
and Mohammadi, Fatemeh
177
and Moradi 194, 198
and Nouri/Shokoufeh
201–2
and Shahidi 139–40, 149
and Tabatabai 164
and Zahtabchi 79
torture 3–4; *see also* white
torture
touch 7
trauma 7–8, 11
trials 17, 75, 81–2, 88, 90, 173
and lack of 6, 108
Tudeh Party 190

Turkmenistan 51, 229

Ukraine International Airline
　　Flight PS752: 231
United Kingdom (UK) xxvi,
　　3, 25, 138, 141
　　and Zaghari-Ratcliffe 103
United Nations xxii
United States of America
　　(USA) 3, 25
Universal House of Justice
　　130–1

Vakilabad Public Prison
　　115–17, 119–22
Vozara Detention Centre
　　83–5, 200, 210

white torture 1–3, 5–6
　　and definition 6–12
　　see also solitary confinement
women xviii, 4, 9–11, 225–7

women guards 24, 44–6, 125,
　　215–17
Women's Association of
　　Tehran xxxiii
women's rights xxxiv

Yadollahi, Shokoufeh 1,
　　199–208, 232
Yaran committee 115, 123

Zaghari-Ratcliffe, Nazanin
　　xxviii, 1, 2, 91–112
Zahtabchi, Ali Asghar 76,
　　86–7
Zahtabchi, Zahra 1, 75–90,
　　229
Zam, Ruhollah xxxi–xxxii
Zanjan 40
Zanjan Prison xv, xvi–xix,
　　xxix–xxx, 47–9
Ziaei, Gholmarza xvi
Zingeris, Emanuelis xxvi